GLACIER
COUNTRY
MOUNT REVELSTOKE AND
GLACIER NATIONAL PARKS

GLACIER COUNTRY

MOUNT REVELSTOKE AND GLACIER NATIONAL PARKS

JOHN G. WOODS

Douglas & McIntyre
Vancouver/Toronto

*Published in co-operation with Environment Canada – Parks
and the Canadian Government Publishing Centre,
Supply and Services Canada*

Copyright © Minister of Supply and Services Canada 1987
Catalogue number R62-150/5-1987E

Douglas & McIntyre Ltd., 1615 Venables Street, Vancouver, British Columbia V5L 2H1

Canadian Cataloguing in Publication Data

Woods, John G.
Glacier Country: Mount Revelstoke and Glacier National Parks

Includes index.
Bibliography: p.
ISBN 0-88894-541-8

   1. Mount Revelstoke National Park (B.C.) – Guide-books.   2. Glacier National Park (B.C.) – Guide-books.   3. Natural history – British Columbia – Mount Revelstoke National Park – Guide-books.   4. Natural history – British Columbia – Glacier National Park – Guide-books.   I. Parks Canada.   II. Title.
FC3814.M69W6 1987   917.11′43 C87-091055-8

Design and Maps by Evelyn Kirkaldy
Frontispiece photograph: Alpine wildflowers, Mount Revelstoke, by John G. Woods

Printed and bound in Canada by D. W. Friesen & Sons Ltd.

Environment   Environnement
Canada   Canada

Parks   Parcs

CONTENTS

PREFACE

My first experience in Glacier Country was a drive taken with my wife Marcia over Rogers Pass in December 1974. It was snowing, and every time we crossed a treeless swath marked "Avalanche Area—No Stopping," we both held our breaths. At one point we were delayed for an hour while avalanches were stabilized above the roadway ahead. The heavy snowfall blocked any chance of seeing the action, but I'll always remember the deep boom of the howitzer echoing along the narrow valley walls and a glimpse of the big cannon as it was hauled past us en route to a new shooting position. The next day the skies partially cleared, and we had our first look at the summits, icefields and deep valleys which would be our new home. Months later we met the man responsible for the world-renowned avalanche control program, V. G. (Fred) Schleiss.

Although I had already worked as the biologist-naturalist in several national and provincial parks, my previous experience in Eastern Canada made me more comfortable in the stern of a canoe than in stiff-soled climbing boots. Now, as the newly appointed Chief Park Naturalist for Mount Revelstoke and Glacier, I faced some of the steepest and wildest mountain terrain on the continent. Fred Schleiss and I immediately became friends and colleagues. Under his expert guidance (he is a world-calibre ski mountaineer, hiker, and climber as well as a foremost avalanche control expert), I was soon probing the backcountry. Fred's encouragement, knowledge and professionalism have inspired me to pursue the exploration of these magnificent mountains, and I would like to acknowledge his central role in helping me feel at home here.

Of course, over the years many others have given this flatlander a hand, sharing their experience in mountain travel and their knowledge of human and natural history. In particular, I would like to thank Dr. P. Achuff, R. Bonar, E. Burn, E. Callin, H. Coneybeare, Dr. M. Dyer, Dr. M. B. Fenton, W. D. Gallacher, M. Gartshore, B. Haggerstone, W. Laurila, O. Lavallée, J. Mulchinock, C. S. C. Ommanney, W. Schleiss, D. Threatful, Dr. J. O. Wheeler, P. Whitfield and M. Woods.

John G. Woods

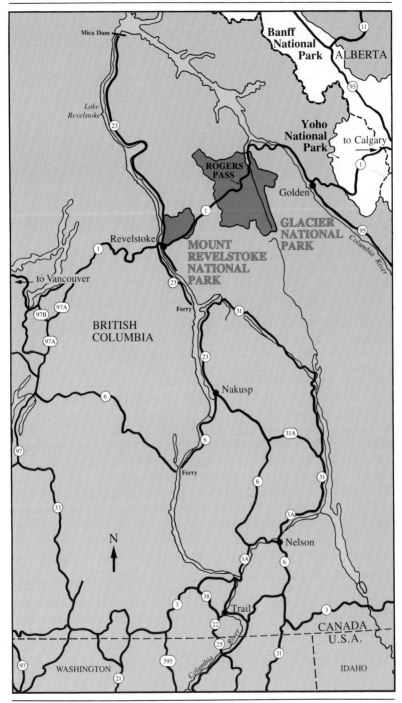

INTRODUCTION

On 10 October 1986 a small group of park visitors and officials assembled at the summit of Rogers Pass to celebrate a landmark in Canadian conservation: the one hundredth birthday of Glacier National Park. Had they been able to slip back in time to 1886, the group would have found themselves standing along the main route of the Canadian Pacific Railway just outside a gigantic wooden snowshed—newly constructed and ready to be tested by the fierce snowslides that make the Columbia Mountains a formidable barrier between the Prairies and the Pacific. History would show that the railway's respect for the danger of avalanches was well-founded; and despite precautions, many lives would be lost in the snowy torrents during the ensuing century.

At the summit of Rogers Pass in 1886 there would have been two railway tracks: one through the shed for winter use and another outside for use in summer. Thus when avalanches did not threaten the line, the trains could run in the open, allowing passengers to experience the magnificent mountain views. And what views! Bold fortresses like Mount Tupper and Mount Macdonald, horns like Mount Sir Donald, and the serrations of Mount Rogers. Glaciers and icefields sprawled down from the skyline, reminding visitors that winter is always on Glacier's doorstep. This combination of bold but symmetrical relief, narrow valleys and moving sheets of ice defined the visual character of the Columbia Mountains and attracted visitors from around the world. In the words of William Van Horne, general manager of the CPR during the construction years, this spot was "the climax of mountain scenery." More adventuresome tourists would have found the deep-clawed tracks of grizzly bears and their smaller relatives, black bears. Hikers of the day recognized that as soon as they stepped away from the railway line they were in real wilderness.

This was the country that became a national park reserve in 1886—an area set aside for all time as representing some of the best of Canada's natural heritage and protected by legislation enacted at the highest level of government. Along with Banff, established the previous year, and Yoho, also in 1886, Glacier became an early member of the world-wide family of national parks. Three decades later, in 1914, another area of the Columbias just west of Glacier was designated Mount Revelstoke National Park. Together, they became Canada's representatives of the Columbia Mountains.

In the years following the establishment of these parks, notions of how to manage national parks matured. At first, mining, logging, hunting and trapping were considered to be compatible with the overall objective of preserving and promoting the scenery. But today national parks have become places where every effort is made to allow the forces of nature a free hand and where visitors are encouraged to enjoy the land on its own terms.

With increased development in the mountains around the parks, the wisdom of saving a portion of the original face of the land has proven itself. Open almost any coffee table book on Western Canada and you will find photographs of the Rogers Pass summits and the alpine flower meadows on Mount Revelstoke. In fact, the tourism industry promotes this magnificent scenery around the world.

As Glacier heads into its second century and Mount Revelstoke approaches its first, we can take pride in what has been accomplished. In the 1349 km² of Glacier and the 259 km² of Mount Revelstoke, unscarred peaks still line the horizon. Most of these forests have never seen an axe or chainsaw, and big bears still wander the slopes. The original railway over Rogers Pass has been abandoned. The line still crosses Glacier park but now runs through tunnels beneath the pass. Today a modern highway brings visitors to the doorstep of wilderness. Hiking trails, picnic areas and campgrounds encourage visitors to spend recreation time here throughout the seasons.

This book is both a primer on the area's rich heritage and a guide to exploring the parks. It is presented with the hope that you will not only enjoy the parks but also join in the continuing effort to keep them unspoiled. As park history unfolds, our challenge is to ensure that future visitors continue to find in this region the climax of mountain scenery.

THE MOUNTAIN MOSAIC

August 21st, 1983—a glorious night to bivouac among the peaks. Low-angled rays from the sun brushed washes of gold, pink and crimson over the icefield below. To the west, the mountain peaks looked like a wind-lashed sea where rock waves buffeted the sky. Perched on narrow nestlike platforms scraped into the side of the mountain, a group of climbers settled into the uneasy sleep that comes from hard work and anticipation of impending adventure. The rock-strewn surface of the glacier was ample proof that Mount Sir Donald, the glacier's backwall and their climbing objective, was a dynamic mountain not to be casually approached. By choosing to spend the night in well-used camping sites, the mountaineers had shown respect.

All day they had tested lungs and muscles against the base of Mount Sir Donald. One thousand metres below they had passed the end-of-trail sign. Higher still, at a late afternoon halt near the toe of Vaux Glacier, they had been given a warning. While they rested, the sun's heat loosened the glacier's surface and sent a shower of rocks bouncing down the steep, crevasse-lined ice face.

Now, as dark gripped the mountains, Sir Donald stirred again and sent a massive landslide ripping down its western face. The main force of the rock avalanche slammed onto the glacier. At the edge of the slide, shattered fragments of Sir Donald riddled the campsite. Rock bullets tore through the tents striking one climber in the leg and narrowly missing others. Dust blotted out the stars as the party scrambled to partial safety at the base of an overhanging cliff. Throughout the night, irregular salvos of rock kept the group in constant uncertainty. In the morning, the climbers retreated from the mountain. As they retraced their route by the Vaux Glacier, they saw an immense quantity of new rock on the glacier's surface, and above the ice, a fresh orange scar on the face of Sir Donald.

Measured in human terms, events such as this rockslide are rare, but measured in the life and death of mountains, they happen constantly. Stand on any good vantage in Mount Revelstoke or Glacier parks and you will see the telltale boulder piles, steep walls and rock-covered glaciers that prove these mountains are actively changing.

When the last great ice age came to an end 10 000 to 15 000 years ago, it had destroyed much of the evidence left by millennia of erosion. Only tiny islands of rock above the glaciers and certain passageways in underground caverns escaped the blade of ice. Gone were the soils, the river gravels, the scree slopes and the rockslides of preglacial times. When you see such products of erosion in the parks today, you are looking at brand new deposits only a fraction of the age of the mountains themselves.

THE MOUNTAIN MYSTERY

Earth scientists are expert detectives who use clues millions of years old to piece together mysteries unwitnessed by humans. Masters of the abstract, they are able to take small pieces from a three-dimensional landscape puzzle, place them in time, and reconstruct the events which led to the formation of the land as we see it today. Anywhere in the world, the story of how the earth formed, moved and was shaped is a story full of wonderful complexity. But the western mountains of North America, where much of the earth stands on end, is a case for the most Sherlockean geologist.

The first to tackle the problems of this mountain geography were the early explorers—the mapmakers. At the start of the nineteenth century, the famous explorer, cartographer and North West Company employee David Thompson circled the area now encompassed by Mount Revelstoke and Glacier National Parks using the Columbia River as his highway. Thompson recognized that these mountains were a unique assemblage. He called them Nelson's Mountains after the famous naval hero of his day. Later, when the Hudson's Bay Company bought out the North West Company, the name was changed to the Selkirks in honour of Lord Thomas Douglas Selkirk, an HBC executive.

In the wake of Thompson's travels came an army of explorers, geographers and scientists. Not content with the view from the river, they probed the valleys, climbed the peaks, and in more recent times took stock of the mountains from the air and by satellite. Although names were added to maps with increasing authority, the basic fact remained: the mountains of which Mount Revelstoke and Glacier are part differ from the Rockies, the Coast Mountains, the Ominecas, the Cascades and the myriad of other vertical landscapes which make the western Cordillera a breathtaking mosaic.

According to the latest maps, the parks are part of the Columbia Mountains, a name related to the fact that the area is largely embraced by the great bending arm of the Columbia River. The Columbias are divided into four main groups: the Selkirks, the Purcells, the Monashees and the Cariboos. Mount Revelstoke National Park is totally within the Selkirks and affords excellent views onto the Monashees. Glacier National Park lies mostly within the Selkirks but includes a delightful strip of the alpine in the Purcells.

If you study topographic maps, another level of mountain naming appears: the mountain range. Ranges such as the Sir Donald Range in Glacier and the Clachnacudainn Range in Mount Revelstoke are groups of mountains linked together because they appear as a visual unit.

The first cartographer to provide detailed topographic maps of these parks was Arthur O. Wheeler. Working in the summers of 1901 and 1902, he scaled many of the peaks within hiking distance of the Canadian Pacific Railway through Rogers Pass. Using photo-topographical methods of surveying called photogrammetry, Wheeler started from a base line of known length and elevation on the railway line near Revelstoke. With a theodolite, he took a series of bearings and vertical angles on the mountains towards Rogers Pass. Precisely oriented photographs taken with a special survey camera supplemented his measurements. He then climbed prominent mountains visible from this base line. After recording the elevation of each new position, Wheeler noted bearings to significant landscape features and carefully photographed the scenery. From point to point, he extended the survey from Revelstoke towards Rogers Pass. Because his camera was precisely positioned for each shot, he could use the photographs to make an additional series of calculations and complete a detailed survey of the landscape.

Wheeler's first challenge—climbing some of the roughest peaks in the west—was formidable; back in Ottawa he faced an equally staggering task of sorting his data. Today's mapmakers have all the benefits of aerial photography and computer-assisted data analysis. Wheeler had none, yet his maps stand as a marvel of accuracy and cartographic skill.

The events leading to our modern topographic maps were the vital first steps in understanding the mystery of these mountains. With good maps in hand, the geologists had the basic tools they needed to investigate the great mystery of how this landscape was formed.

FROM SEA TO SEA

In 1890 Dr. George M. Dawson presented a learned paper describing the Selkirks to the Geological Society of America. Like a convention of sleuths, the geologists spoke to each other in the coded language of their science. Dawson described the rocks of the Selkirks as ''quite schistose, hornblendic, with graphitic tendencies. . . .'' Nearly a century later, geologists still make their studies difficult to comprehend when they speak of the ''Omineca crystalline belt'' and ''allochthonous composite terranes.''

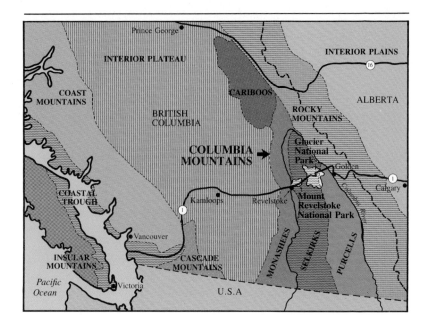

But as complex as the story of the mountains is, thanks to these geological detectives it is now possible to describe some basic principles about how the mountains you see in Mount Revelstoke and Glacier came to be.

Three generations after A. O. Wheeler produced the first good topographical maps of this area in 1904, his grandson, Dr. John O. Wheeler, tackled the geological mapping of the Columbia Mountains as part of the systematic survey of the geology of Canada. This time, with the assistance of helicopters and aerial photographs, he identified the rock types exposed in the parks and plotted them on detailed maps. By studying the few fossils found in the rocks, and measuring the radioactive decay of certain minerals in them, he determined their age. He located the major faults that disrupt the rock formations and investigated the shapes of the folds found in the rock layers. His final geological maps show the composition, distribution and configuration of rock formations underlying both parks. These maps allowed scientists to better understand the geological evolution of the region and its role in the building of the mountains of western North America.

When you look at the exposed rock on the face of Mounts Tupper and Macdonald you can see that the rocks were once laid down in layers. Closer examination reveals them to be largely quartzite and slates, rocks known to originate as deposits of sand and mud. From this evidence we deduce that the rocks must have been formed under water. In fact, these sedimentary rocks were deposited nearly 600 million years ago on a broad,

Layered bedrock of Mount Tupper, Rogers Pass

shallow shelf along the western margin of what was then North America. Long meandering rivers snaked across this low-lying ancient continent and carried sand and silt onto the continental shelf much as today the Mississippi River carries sediment to the Gulf of Mexico.

Occasionally the seas retreated and the sediments were eroded. At other times the waters were warm and harboured reefs of living coral and sponges. Lime from the bodies of these creatures became layers of limestone such as are exposed near Cougar Brook in Glacier park. These sediments were deposited over millions of years, a period of deposition nearly unfathomable to the human mind. Also staggering is the thickness of accumulated sediment: about 4.5 km of sedimentary rocks are exposed in Glacier and another 10 km of sediments underlie these rocks in the southern Purcell Mountains.

More mental gymnastics are needed to imagine solid rock twisting, tilting and folding. But the great folds on Cougar Mountain and Mount Macdonald are proof that something has lifted and deformed the sediments. Beginning about 185 million years ago the bedrock slowly rose out of the sea. According to current theory, first one great area of land then another rafted across the Pacific Ocean and pushed against the west coast of North America. During the first collision, the sediments which would become the Columbia Mountains buckled, and a belt of flat-lying rock 300 km wide became a band of mountains 150 km across. This gradual compression of the landscape sent some of the rocks into the lower crust of the earth to depths of 20 to 25 km and locally even into the molten mantle beneath.

Other sections of rock were thrust skyward to form mountains. Awesome pressures and heat, generated by depressing the formations into the earth's crust and by loading them under stacks of overthrust sheets of rock, recrystallized sandstone into quartzite. Mudstone became shale and slate; limestone turned into marble. These hardened, metamorphosed rocks now form the spectacular summits of the Selkirks.

The distorted layers of rock we see throughout the two parks offer dramatic evidence of a chaotic past. As they adjusted to the increased pressures, the rocks were bent into folds and broken faults, probably accompanied by earthquakes. Major river valleys such as that now occupied by the Beaver and Columbia rivers originated as fault lines. Veins of white quartz snaking through the rock layers are signs that these rocks once cracked and were invaded by mineral-rich liquids.

When you talk to geologists about the history of Mount Revelstoke National Park, they often acknowledge that it is a truly hard case to solve. The park represents a slice of deeper, more recrystallized rocks intruded by granitic masses. These masses were crystallized from molten material at different times: 375 and 110 million years ago. The Mount Revelstoke rocks are separated by a fault along the Columbia River valley from sheets of older Precambrian metamorphic rocks that once formed the basement rocks of North America but have since been brought to the surface to form the adjacent Monashee Mountains.

As a general rule, the older the mountains, the more deeply hidden their story. While the mountains of Mount Revelstoke and Glacier have the distinction of being part of the original Cordillera, time and weathering have obscured much of their past.

The shapes of the mountains in Mount Revelstoke and Glacier parks are influenced by the nature of the rocks which form them. As the rock formations were uplifted, erosion by water, ice and, to a lesser extent, wind wore them down. In areas of outcropping quartzite (composed largely of resistant quartz grains) and limestone (formed from the shells of ancient sea creatures), the mountains create bold landscapes and form the highest peaks. Dramatic peaks such as Sir Donald, Tupper and Rogers are capped with these resistant formations. Where weaker slates reach the surface, the landscape has eroded to the more subdued outlines you see in the Bald Mountain and Flat Creek areas of Glacier.

As part of their scientific shorthand, geologists have named these major rock groups — usually after the place where they first described a distinctive assemblage of rocks. Thus they speak of the "Hamill" group featuring quartzites, the limestones of the "Badshot Formation," the slates of the "Horsethief Creek and Lardeau" groups and the highly varied area of rocks they lump together as the "Shuswap Metamorphic Complex."

JOHN G. WOODS

Headwaters of the Beaver River

Since these mountains are ancient, and erosion has been wearing them down for a long time, why haven't they disappeared altogether? At the same time that some of the original ocean sediments were thrust up, other folds were pushed down. These buried rocks tend to be lighter than the surrounding material. As erosion strips rocks from the mountains, the weight on the buried layers decreases, and they can rebound slightly towards the surface. Only when either the folding or the rebound ends will erosion erase the mountains; then the rivers will complete their task of carrying the Columbias back to the sea.

THE UPS AND DOWNS OF MOUNTAIN RIVERS
Geomorphologists—earth scientists who study the shape of the land —generally agree that the valleys occupied by ice age glaciers were first eroded by rivers. In this area of the Cordillera, the mountains intercept great quantities of moisture rolling in from the Pacific Ocean. Abundant water and steep terrain combine to produce powerful streams capable of moving large quantities of rock debris. Listen to the sound of large boulders bouncing down a muddy, turbulent streambed on a hot summer day and you will get a sense of this power.

Carbonate Grotto, Nakimu Caves

Fueled by meltwater from the glaciers and snowfields, the streams have two periods of peak flow: the spring flood when the snow leaves the low country, then the summer peak when heat releases meltwater from the high-elevation snowpack and ice. As glaciers scrape the bedrock, tiny fragments of rock choke these summer floodwaters, turning them milky white. You can often detect a low hiss as these fine fragments collide in the murky waters. In quiet eddies, a thick white paste of this ''rock flour'' collects on boulders.

The direct relation between river flow and glacier melt can often be seen during clear, summer weather. Under starry skies, air temperatures drop, and glacial melt is reduced. With less meltwater charging their veins, stream levels drop and by early morning they achieve minimum daily flows. As sun warms the air in the mountains, meltwater from the glaciers increases. By late afternoon a stream which was a quiet trickle at 7:00 A.M. can be transformed into a torrent.

While rivers such as the Illecillewaet and Beaver put on an impressive show of power each summer, occasionally a combination of warm weather and heavy rainfall turns them into awesome agents of erosion. Beached snags and gravel bars in the forest far from any stream testify to the fact that large-scale flooding, like large rockslides, is not unusual in these mountains.

During July 1983, warm, heavy rains sent rivers in the parks above their banks. As river after river swelled, huge trees growing along the watercourses were undercut and toppled into the froth. Exposed banks crumbled, and torrents cut new paths through the forests. The floodwaters undermined bridges and ate into roadbeds along both the Trans-Canada Highway and the Canadian Pacific Railway. Trains and highway traffic came to a halt. In human terms, the flood was a disaster meriting national attention. But from the perspective of the natural world, the flood was taken in stride. Through the ages, events like this have helped carve the mountain landscape.

RIVERS OF DARKNESS

In at least two places in Glacier park, rivers have not only carved the surface of the mountains but also have found their way underground and riddled the bedrock with interconnecting passageways and caverns. Like other landscapes in the parks, these subterranean voids are active and constantly changing.

Nakimu, the larger of the two, and one of Canada's longest cave systems, boasts of more than 5 km of passageways. The thunder of moving water echoes in Nakimu's perpetual night as Cougar Brook courses through the caves, tumbles in unseen cascades and plummets over waterfalls which have never sparkled in the sun.

Unlike the quartzites, slates and other metamorphic rocks seen as outcrops over most of Mount Revelstoke and Glacier, the limestone of these areas is relatively soluble when exposed to acidic water. A weak carbonic acid is formed when carbon dioxide in the air and soil mixes with surface water. By infiltrating cracks in the limestone, groundwater can corrode the bedrock and eventually form passageways capable of channelling a stream's entire flow. Charged with abrasive sand and gravel from surface erosion, the underground rivers pound the cavern walls and cut deeply into the limestone. This process also creates quarry-sized holes on the surface of extensive areas of limestone. Such pitted topography is referred to as karst.

Rumours of cave systems connecting over wide stretches of these mountains were once rife. But detailed studies conducted at Nakimu in the 1960s by Dr. Derek Ford of McMaster University show that while the caves are remarkable in size and form, they are restricted to the Badshot limestone in the Cougar Brook valley. Ford's studies also reveal that Nakimu is one of the oldest landscapes in these mountains; some of the passageways existed before the last great ice age came to an end.

EXPLORING THE PARKS' GEOLOGY

The Trans-Canada Highway and Mount Revelstoke Summit Road provide excellent views of the parks' landscape. Starting at the north boundary of Glacier, the highway runs up the valley of the Beaver River which flows in the Purcell Trench—a fault line separating the Purcells from the Selkirks. From viewpoints in the Beaver valley you can compare the rugged landscape of the Selkirks to the west with the more subdued landscape of the Purcells to the east. The surface bedrock in this area of the Selkirks is largely the weather-resistent quartzites of the Hamill Group. The more rounded appearance of the Purcells is a reflection of softer bedrock —principally slate belonging to the Horsethief Creek Group.

Continuing westbound, you enter Rogers Pass. To the north, the fortress of the Hermit Range looms above the highway. To the south, the peaks of the Sir Donald Range guard the pass. Note that the highway is forced onto the side walls of Rogers Pass. After leaving the pass, watch for a large rockslide of Hamill quartzite on the north side of the highway.

Near the west boundary of Glacier, you will note that the landscape takes on a different character. While still in the Selkirks, you have entered the Lardeau Group of bedrock. Here slates and schist produce a landscape similar to the Purcells on Glacier's eastern boundary.

When you reach the boundary of Mount Revelstoke, you are well within an area in which a variety of metamorphic and granitic rocks produce a varied landscape. In the Clachnacudainn Creek area the topography is extremely rugged. By driving up the park's Summit Road, you will see a more gentle version of this complex area. The Summit Road also offers outstanding vistas of the Columbia River valley and the Monashees to the west.

While there are numerous rock cuts along both parks' roads, visitors are reminded that all natural features must be left untouched. A detailed guide to the geology as seen from the Trans-Canada can be ordered from the Geological Survey of Canada, Vancouver. See R. A. Price et al. in the Suggested Reading list, p. 124.

Although park caves are closed to the general public, the surface features of a karst landscape are evident along the Cougar Brook trail. In the Rogers Pass Information Centre there is a life-scale replica of part of the cave system. The movie *Underground Rivers,* shown in the Centre's theatre, takes you into the subterranean world of Nakimu Caves.

HIGH PEAKS OF MOUNT REVELSTOKE AND GLACIER

Mountain	Park	Elevation (m)	Geological Group
Moonraker	Glacier	2841	Horsethief Creek
Silent	Glacier	2670	Horsethief Creek
Copperstain	Glacier	2609	Horsethief Creek
Dawson	Glacier	3390	Hamill
Wheeler	Glacier	3363	Hamill
Selwyn	Glacier	3360	Hamill
Grand	Glacier	3305	Hamill
Kilpatrick	Glacier	3238	Hamill
Sir Donald	Glacier	3297	Hamill
Corbin	Glacier	2712	Lardeau
Coursier	Mount Revelstoke	2646	Shuswap
Klotz	Mount Revelstoke	2643	Shuswap
Dickey	Mount Revelstoke	2518	Shuswap

LIVING ICE

"Is it a real glacier, or only one
the company has put here for an advertisement?"
Park visitor, circa 1900

G lacial gravel deposits, displaced boulders and scratched bedrock are silent reminders of a time when moving ice covered most of Canada. But in Mount Revelstoke and Glacier national parks, there is no need to stretch your imagination to hear the deep vibrations of moving ice or feel the chilling winds of an ice-age summer. Here, more than 400 glaciers still cover a tenth of the landscape.

Life for these glaciers comes from the sky. An infinity of snowflakes sifts onto the mountain slopes each autumn blanketing first the summits and then the valleys. By March, snows on the high slopes are deep enough to hide a cabin. As spring becomes summer, warm temperatures attack the snowpack and chase it up the mountain. In most of Canada, this seasonal thaw obliterates all signs of winter. But here, as you climb uphill, the air cools and the snows deepen. Before you reach the summits, the battle between sun and snow can shift. Wherever snowflakes survive from one winter to the next, a glacier is born.

Anyone who has packed a snowball has had some experience with the forces that change delicate snowflakes into powerful sheets of grinding ice. When snow first falls, it is so lightly packed that it consists mostly of air. Gravity, acting like your fingers on a snowball, compacts the crystals; air is squeezed out of the snowpack, and the fragile starlike snowflakes lose shape and identity. Although this happens to some extent at the bottom of the yearly snowpack, the snows from hundreds of winters must persist to form a glacier. No one knows just how thick our glaciers are, but guesses in the 100-metre range are not far-fetched.

Snow in these mountains can cling and accumulate on extremely steep slopes, but the usual places for glaciers to form are the natural high basins between the peaks. These are the snowfields, icefields and névés shown on park maps. Avalanches from the steeper pitches bring even more snow onto the glacial spawning beds. In these basins the snows from many

---

Grand Glacier, Glacier National Park   JOHN G. WOODS

JOHN G. WOODS

Shallow crevasses in the Beaver Glacier

winters layer the glaciers and give the ice life. Just as gravity once pulled the snowflakes to earth, the same force attracts the deepening glaciers. Overflowing their mountain cradles, they send moving arms of ice creeping towards the valleys.

Although we usually think of ice as a solid, under the right conditions of temperature and pressure it is capable of plastic flow. Glacial ice gliding down slope moves by a rearrangement and restructuring of its crystals, and by slipping along its contact with the mountain. The deep vibrations occasionally heard coming from glacial ice are evidence of this movement. Like water in a river, the ice flows fastest at the surface and in midstream. Measured in terms of a few centimetres or metres a day, these ice rivers move slowly in comparison with their watery counterparts, but they have the advantage of mass.

Where the moving ice flows over gentle or concave terrain, the ice is solid and the surface smooth. If you were to cross an icefield in these areas, you would encounter a desertlike scene with dunes of snow-covered ice rounding the landscape. But where the glacier tumbles down steep inclines and over cliffs, the gentleness is lost in a chaos of crevasses, icefalls and caves. Forced by the steep slopes to accelerate, the ice loses its ability to adjust to changing pressures, and its brittle character is revealed. Crevasses reaching 50 to 100 m into the ice may open up as the ice extends itself over the steepening terrain. Seen from a distance, these giant cracks distinguish a glacier from just another patch of snow. In winter many of these crevasses are bridged by snow, but in summer the bridges weaken and can disappear. A chief danger in crossing a snow-covered glacier comes from the possibility of falling through one of these weakened bridges and into a crevasse.

In places crevasses crisscross and form seemingly impenetrable fields of ice pinnacles known as seracs. At the head of a glacier, at its uppermost contact with the mountain, a special crevasse, the bergschrund, makes travel difficult for climbers. Where glaciers hang on steep hillsides and push out over cliffs, great masses of ice can suddenly break away from the parent glaciers and cascade into the valleys. You can hear the deep roar of these ice avalanches throughout the summer in the Dawson Range of Glacier park.

Rockslides rumble down from the cliffs above the ice and add debris to its surface. One glacier in the southern portion of the Purity Range was so widely covered by rockslide debris that it was referred to as the Dirty Glacier. Now its official name is the Black Glacier. In the headwaters of Grizzly Creek, another glacier has become completely covered by boulders and is one of the few examples within the parks of a rock glacier.

MASTER CARVERS

During their downward movement, glaciers take a hand in shaping the landscape. The moving ice plucks boulders from the bedrock and carries them along. Now part of the life of the glacier, these rocks push against each other and scrape away at the mountains. Unseen, they chatter across buried ridges and sculpt the bedrock with crescents and grooves. The fine rock powder produced by this grinding gives glacial meltwaters their characteristic milky appearance in summer.

Streams of meltwater can lace the lower reaches of a glacier during the warmest months of the year. Rivulets often cross the ice for a way, then plunge into a crevasse. Swirling waters moving through the ice create smooth-walled passageways and plunging holes called millwells. Such a stream may continue beneath the ice, often showing a hollowed tube where it re-emerges at the snout of the glacier.

Moving into the valleys, glacial ice enters a hostile environment of increasing warmth. In its highest reaches a glacier may always have some snow cover, but at lower elevations the winter snow melts, and the sun can attack the ice directly. The lower the glacier moves, the greater the melting until at last it can reach no farther. Here the glacier pushes its snout to the limit, but it only seems to have stopped. If new ice does not constantly flow from above, the glacier's snout will retreat up slope. If the melting decreases, the snout will push even farther into the valley.

Along the margins of the glacier we see evidence of movement and erosion. Large boulders melt out and are piled along a static ice edge. In time these rocks build up to form lateral moraines—the conspicuous gravel ridges you can see beside many of our parks' glaciers. Where a glacier has temporarily retreated, it reveals a landscape of scratched, gouged and polished bedrock.

On a larger scale, the great power of glaciers is seen in the many sharp peaks, knife-edged ridges, armchair basins and U-shaped valleys in the parks. When you look at Mount Sir Donald from Illecillewaet Campground in Glacier National Park, you are treated to a view of a classic Matterhorn-type mountain. Horns like Sir Donald are formed by glaciers eating away at the mountain from all directions, increasingly steepening its sides and isolating it from other peaks. The same process sharpens ridges when glaciers grind away on only two sides. Many of the ridges in the Hermit Range illustrate these arêtes when viewed from the summit of Rogers Pass. Cirques are formed by the presence of a glacier in a natural depression. Over time the glacier deepens the bowl and steepens its walls. Throughout the parks countless cirques mark the slopes. Some of these cirques still contain their glaciers; others are evidence of an icier time in our past.

THE PENDULUM OF CHANGE

When you consider how changeable the climate in these parks is from year to year, it should come as no surprise that glaciers rarely remain constant in size. A glacier can be said to operate on a budget. When a glacier's income of snow exceeds its expenditures of melt, its icy wealth increases; when melt overspends the supply of ice, the glacier shrinks. A cold summer can contribute to a positive glacial budget, as can a snowy winter. Warm summers and dry winters tip the budget into the red, and the glaciers retreat to higher positions in the mountains.

Scientists have pieced together part of the glacial history for these mountains stretching back at least a thousand centuries. During the age of perpetual winter, most of Canada was covered by continental ice sheets. But here, the highest peaks protruded above the ice—islands in a frozen, moving sea. These nunataks, like the summit of Mount Sir Donald, were extreme environments subjected to the full force of cold and wind.

Burial by ice several kilometres thick had profound influences on the landscape we see in the parks today. Glacial erosion widened the sides of the valleys, giving them a characteristic U-shape. The ice overran most of the lower summits, such as the summit of Mount Revelstoke, and rounded them in the process. Any life that had existed before the ice age was forced from the mountains.

With a warming trend 10 000 to 15 000 years ago, the glaciers began to recede. Large amounts of meltwater formed glacial lakes and streams. The rocks and boulders eroded by millennia of icy excavation were reworked and deposited in thick beds in many areas. Ten thousand years later these same sands and gravels supplied construction materials for the railway and highway that now traverse the parks.

Glaciers continue to sculpt the Sir Donald Range

Five thousand years ago there were likely very few, if any, glaciers in the parks. Although the mountains looked much as they do today, they lacked the characteristic snowiness we have come to associate with the Columbias. The pendulum of climate had swung from cold to warm and was poised for change.

In the millennia following the glacial minimum, the mountains returned to snowy winters and cooler summers, and the snows once again persisted in high alpine pockets. Reaching down slope, they obliterated the plants and animals in their paths but did not regain their full domination on the land. In this neoglacial period or "little ice age," the glaciers nosed down to an elevation of about 1400 m. When tourists first visited this area a century ago, this little ice age was at its peak.

With the completion of the Canadian Pacific Railway in 1885, tourists flocked to the area and marvelled at the combination of snow and ice which had created some of the best scenery on earth. But even though the land was at its snowy best since the great age of ice, it soon became apparent that each year the glaciers were growing smaller.

In 1887 members of the adventuresome Vaux family from Philadelphia made their first visit to Glacier and started detailed studies on the Illecillewaet and Asulkan glaciers. During the next thirty years, they chronicled the retreat of these great masses of ice using photographs, tarred rocks and markers. Great expanses of bare rock left in the wake of the dwindling ice provided even casual visitors with vivid proof that the park was losing its icy cover.

Man (extreme foreground) dwarfed by the Vaux Glacier

When the Trans-Canada Highway was completed in 1962, a second wave of tourists swarmed into these mountains. By then the glaciers had visibly receded, and most people concluded that the ice was in retreat. But ten years later when a group of park naturalists reactivated surveys on the Illecillewaet Glacier, using the standard procedure of placing a series of markers in front of the glacier's snout and annually measuring the distance from each marker to the ice, they were surprised to discover that the snout of the glacier was once again advancing. Where it had been easy to walk onto the ice a few years earlier, the glacier's front had steepened, become more crevassed and bulged down slope. Instead of measuring a continual retreat from the markers, the ice bulldozed three of them beneath its moving surface within the first year of the study. In the years from 1972 to 1986, the glacier bulged more each year.

In the southern part of the Beaver River valley, the lowest glacier in Glacier park was also showing signs of enlargement; by 1978 it was over-riding alder shrubs growing in its path. A study of Glacier park's 422 glaciers by Environment Canada's National Hydrology Research Institute showed a 14 per cent increase in area of ice between 1951 and 1978 as well as steeper, more active ice fronts.

Although little work has been done on glacial history in Mount Revelstoke, the Woolsey Glacier received special attention during the years 1965 to 1975. In contrast to the Illecillewaet during this period, the Woolsey showed signs of continuing retreat. Large blocks of ice were buried in debris left by the shrinking glacier. These blocks melted slowly and often left large caves in the glacial drift. Although it is not known whether the

Woolsey is still in retreat, this variability in timing of glacial response illustrates the complexity of studying glaciers in the mountains. Like the snowflakes which once formed them, each glacier is unique.

VIEWING PARK GLACIERS

The best time to view park glaciers is late July through early September. For much of the year the glaciers are buried in so much fresh snow that it is difficult to see the ice. From the highway, use binoculars and look for telltale crevasses.

As you drive through Glacier National Park, several glaciers can be easily seen although none is at road level. At the north boundary sign, a small viewpoint features several glaciers plastered on the eastern walls of the Hermit and Sir Donald ranges. The most southern glacier is a good example of a hanging glacier — one perched at an impossibly steep angle on a mountain face. Looking down the Beaver valley you can see the broad U-shape left from times when glaciers flowed down the main valley. Various horns, arêtes and cirques also can be seen from here.

Partway up the ascent into Rogers Pass, a viewpoint on the south side of the highway provides a vista onto the less snowy Purcells. These mountains are partially in the snow shadow of the Selkirks and are of generally lower elevation. Although glaciers are fewer in this part of the park, evidence of past glaciation is obvious in the smoothed landforms. Below you, quarries opened during construction of the highway reveal the depth of glacial gravels deposited during the close of the last major ice age.

The best place to see glaciers along the Trans-Canada Highway is at the summit of Rogers Pass. Here a viewpoint on the west side of the highway features signs naming the mountains and several of the major glaciers.

If you yearn to examine glacial ice at close hand, several park glaciers are within hiking range. As you climb higher in the park, you will discover that the view from the valleys shows misleadingly little ice. For the best overall glacier views, take the Abbott Ridge, Glacier Crest or Avalanche Crest trails. (See Hiking Trails section beginning on p. 81.)

The Great Glacier Trail (p. 93) enables you to hike right to a glacier, although you will have to do a bit of off-trail scrambling. From the trail end, follow the bedrock uphill towards the icefront, picking your own route. When you near the ice, keep well back from the centre of the toe. You will probably see where large blocks of ice are breaking away and creating dangerous conditions below. Easy access to glacial ice can also be made from the trail ends of the Perley Rock, Sir Donald, Asulkan and Hermit trails (pp. 91,92,94,99). Remember to treat all of these locations with respect — active ice fronts frequently avalanche without warning.

The ultimate experience in glacial country is to cross an ice mass on foot. But only people skilled in the special mountaineering skills necessary

Crossing the Illecillewaet Névé

to cross glaciers safely are encouraged to do this. The basic technique is for a party of climbers to team up and attach themselves at several points to a common rope. If one climber unexpectedly falls through a snow bridge into a crevasse, roped companions can check the fall. Sets of metal spikes, called crampons, strapped onto hiking boots give glacier travellers traction on steep portions of ice. Ice axes are used for a variety of purposes including stopping falls and chopping steps. See pp. 68 and 69 for mountaineering regulations.

Although about 8 per cent of Mount Revelstoke park is covered by glaciers, they are harder to approach than in Glacier park, and none can be easily reached by trail. For glacier views, drive up the Summit Road. As you ascend, several glaciers are visible on the slopes across the Columbia River valley to the west. At the end of the road, a ten-minute hike will take you to a fire tower and viewpoint on the summit knoll where signs point out several features of the landscape including glaciers. The mountains within this park show many obvious signs of recent glaciation, but few glaciers can be seen. However, you can see Gordon Glacier from the north end of Eva Lake and glacial ice on Mount Coursier from the Jade lakes. A small area of permanent ice and snow along Mountain Meadows Trail in the summit area, popularly called The Icebox, is actually a small glacier or glacieret.

Visitors with considerable mountaineering skills might want to plan an expedition to the Woolsey Glacier at the north end of the Clachnacudainn Icefield. The "thermokarst" features at the Woolsey snout are unusual and fascinating examples of glacial deposits. Consult the Mount Revelstoke park warden before undertaking this trip.

RECENT CHANGES IN GLACIER ICE AREAS
in km²

Glacier	1850	1951	1978
Geikie	16.43	15.16	15.43
Deville	15.41	12.16	11.83
Grand	10.79	8.50	8.30
Van Horne*	10.00	7.28	7.52
Illecillewaet	9.27	6.70	6.78
Beaver	9.10	7.20	8.17
Deville Névé	8.92	7.15	7.60
Bonney	7.68	6.28	6.39
Asulkan	5.75	3.28	4.02

* includes both sections of Van Horne Glacier

WHEN THE SNOW
SPEAKS

For Fred Schleiss and his brother Walter, the days leading up to 8 January 1966 had been worrisome. As the heads of the Snow Research and Avalanche Warning Section (SRAWS), these park employees directed the world's largest mobile avalanche control program. On paper their job was straightforward: analyze weather and snowpack conditions, predict periods of avalanche activity, and stabilize avalanche slopes to reduce the hazard for motorists travelling the Trans-Canada Highway through Rogers Pass. In reality their task involved outguessing nature in one of the most complex and changeable landscapes on earth.

So it was that when a blast of wind hit the trailer, shaking the walls and jarring Fred from a much-needed but uneasy sleep, he instantly recognized the danger and reached for the phone connecting his sleeping quarters with the avalanche control centre. One thousand metres above his home in Rogers Pass, the same wind would be loading an arsenal of gullies with deadly charges of blowing snow.

The wind came from the south, over the wide icefield of the Illecillewaet Glacier, and funnelled into Rogers Pass accompanied by the lethal combination of rapidly rising temperatures and high humidity. At the Macdonald West Shoulder Observatory, the howling storm overpowered the automated weather sensors and sent an unreadable scribble across the air velocity chart. At a minimum, the sustained velocities were in the same league as a hurricane—more than 160 km/h. Scouring across the wide front of Avalanche Crest, the wind drifted snow into a battery of four lee-slope gullies lining the western shoulder of Mount Macdonald. Within minutes, the trigger points—critical areas at the top of avalanche paths where snowslides often start—were primed.

When viewed from the air, a fifth of the landscape in Glacier is scarred with treeless swaths stretching from timberline to the valley floor. To people unfamiliar with the mountains, these paths through the timber look like ski runs. In fact, they mark the routes followed by snowslides during the winter months. No one has tallied the total number of these avalanche paths in the parks, but 160 targets are mapped on avalanche defence plans for the small area of Glacier traversed by the Trans-Canada Highway.

If you combine heavy snowfall with steep terrain you have the basic ingredients for an avalanche. In the central Selkirks, the steep-walled slopes and frequent snowstorms create a natural spawning ground for snowslides. The complex array of peaks and valleys combined with ever-changing weather patterns, can give an avalanche forecaster nightmares. Even with the lastest sensing devices, the forecasters admit that their work is only 65 per cent technical analysis; the remainder is based on intuition gained from years of experience in avalanche country.

At strategic points on the mountain slopes, a network of automated sensing stations gathers vital weather information and relays the data into the SRAWS control centre in Rogers Pass. Printers at the observatory display readings of air temperature, wind speed and direction, precipitation and relative humidity. No one factor taken alone is either good or bad for avalanche formation: the skill and art in avalanche forecasting comes from correctly interpreting a multitude of factors affecting the slopes.

When snow blankets the mountains each winter, it lays down a dynamic cover of ice crystals. Not only is each snowflake unique in its fine detail, but differing conditions during the flake's formation lead to numerous categories of snowflake shapes. For example, in the central Selkirks classic snowflakes called stars commonly fall on the slopes. These many-armed crystals may interlock as they spiral from the sky, forming large feathers of snow sliding through the air. Under conditions of high humidity, stars have an impressive ability to cling to steep slopes and can build up a snowpack in areas where other snowflake types would simply slide away as they hit the ground.

During storms, rising air temperatures and turbulent winds may transform stellar crystals into graupel—rounded nuggets of snow with little ability to cling together. If the temperature falls, flakes resembling needles or plates can loosely carpet the slopes. Another pulse in the storm can send a layer of stars on top of the weaker crystal types. When the load on these fragile layers becomes too great, the top layers of snow can suddenly slide away and start an avalanche.

As the winter snowpack develops, the snow settles and the crystals begin a metamorphosis in shape and strength. Usually this settlement makes the snow more stable. However, under certain conditions new weak layers of snow can form under the snowpack and provide a sliding surface for an avalanche.

At manned observatories on Mount Fidelity and at Rogers Pass, avalanche observers take weather readings and perform several tests on snow-

JAMES W. MULCHINOCK

105 mm howitzer used to stabilize avalanche slopes

pack stability. For example, in a shear test they may identify a failure plane in the snowpack and measure its strength. When avalanche conditions are suspected, they may blast small test slopes with hand-thrown charges and patrol the highway to study well-known slidepaths. Fracture lines and sliding snow help confirm the predicted instability of the snow. The results from these tests are immediately relayed to Rogers Pass. Years of experience allow the avalanche forecasters to relate this information to the potential avalanche activity of slidepaths reaching the highway.

All members of the avalanche control team need to be excellent ski mountaineers: they must be able to climb up the slopes and take detailed weather and snowpack readings. These mobile research teams may be directed to dig snow profiles within metres of known avalanche trigger zones. By digging into the snowpack, they can study the crystal structure, temperature, hardness and other factors which lead to avalanches. They often can obtain valuable clues to possible avalanche danger just by noticing the behaviour and feel of the snow as they ski.

Wind contributes to avalanche formation by picking up the snow crystals from one slope, and depositing them on another. This windblown snow can quickly form thick, soft slabs of dangerously unstable snow, and on the morning of 8 January this condition was exactly what worried avalanche control in Rogers Pass. The first days of January that year had been difficult ones for the members of the team. As successive waves of snow blanketed the mountains, the highway was closed and an attempt to reduce the avalanche threat by artillery fire was made.

The object of these stabilization shoots is to bring the dangerous snow down under controlled conditions while the highway is safely closed. The avalanche forecasters direct a special detachment of the Canadian Armed Forces in the bombardment of critical slidepaths. They position a 105-mm howitzer on circular concrete pads at several locations along the highway. A permanent target stake to one side of each gun position provides a point of reference allowing the gun to be precisely aimed at avalanche trigger points under any conditions. The crews frequently must shoot when they cannot see the avalanche paths because of darkness or stormy weather.

In a successful shoot, the howitzer delivers an explosive head into the trigger zone. Shock waves cause the upper layers of snow to break away along a failure plane of weaker snow. As the snowslide moves down, it gathers speed and momentum and sets snow in lower regions of the track in motion. With unstable snow removed from the slopes, the highway can then be safely reopened.

However, when the snow is very loose, instead of breaking away as a slab when the cannon shell explodes, the avalanche can be limited to a small area starting from a single point. These point avalanches affect very small areas and do not stabilize the snowpack.

The cold conditions during the first days of January 1966 had retarded settlement, and waist-deep loose snow lay on the slopes. Despite intensive bombardment in preceding days to stabilize the snowpack, the Schleiss brothers knew that conditions could deteriorate rapidly, aggravated by the lashing winds.

Fifteen minutes after the wind first shrieked into Rogers Pass, all traffic was stopped at the west gate of Mount Revelstoke park and the east gate of Glacier park. However, a few vehicles could have passed through the gates just before the closure. It would take them an hour to drive through the danger zone. Although protected from some snowslides by a series of reinforced concrete sheds, and from others by man-made mounds, dams and dikes, vehicles caught between the two gates would still have to run the gauntlet of avalanche paths normally stabilized by gun fire.

Ten minutes after the gates closed, snow in the most southern gully—Macdonald West Shoulder No. 4—released naturally and blocked the highway between the summit monument and the park compound. Within minutes, a snowslide from the next gully, No. 3, hit the highway. With 234 m of highway smothered by these uncontrolled slides, it was feared that vehicles still travelling between the two gates may have been buried. A rescue team was dispatched to the site to probe for trapped vehicles. The searchers were warned that there could be additional slides from the remaining two gullies and the opposite side of the valley. They were to keep a sharp lookout on the slopes above.

By 9:30, park forces were operating under a "red form"—an operational code indicating closure of the highway for avalanche control. High winds, snowfall and mild temperatures were continuing to make the remaining gullies lethal avenues for the snowy torrents—they required immediate stabilization. Independent of the rescue search, a bulldozer and then a front-end loader arrived at the place where avalanches buried the highway and began to clear a cut through the downed avalanches to allow passage of the gun.

At 10:53, a loud snap cracked through the air, and Fred looked up to see snow gully in No.2 releasing. He reached for his two-way radio and yelled a warning to all personnel in the slide area. Meanwhile, the rescue team had seen the snow break and were running for a safe area they had earmarked in the event of danger.

As the avalanche gathered size and strength, it billowed up like a giant cumulous cloud rushing down the slope. Blending with the fierce winds, the hiss of moving snow became a rumble, then a thunderous roar as tonnes of snow careered towards the highway. Nearing the valley bottom, the compressed air preceding the slide blasted into a thin strip of forest. Snow now moving at 225 km/h uprooted trees and whirled them into the torrent. Wave after wave of snow piled onto the road. Ninety seconds after the first snap, 244 m of highway had disappeared under 2.4 m of avalanche debris. For an additional 18 m, the avalanche had overlapped a previous slide at the point where the bulldozer and loader had been working moments before.

When the snow settled, there was no sign of the big machines. Before the rescue could be completed, the control team had to stabilize the remaining snow above the accident site. Although the howitzer was trapped on the wrong side of the slide for normal stabilization, the control team was able to fire at the slopes from an improvised location. When the line of rescuers started probing the heavy slide debris with flexible metal rods, they soon located the loader. It had been overturned by the air blast and one wheel was just below the surface. After two and a half hours of grim digging, the lifeless body of the driver was removed from the snow. The bulldozer and its operator were still hidden under the great mass of concrete-hard snow.

Continuing high winds and snowfall relentlessly charged the slopes as the rescue team worked. With the approach of dark, the search was called off for fear of more slides down the gullies. Later, the control team was able to partially stabilize the threatening slopes, and the search for the bulldozer operator resumed. At 19:45, twelve hours from the time the killer wind hit the pass, a second body was lifted from the tragic scene.

The next morning the forecasters made a new evaluation of the avalanche hazard and found that cold temperatures during the night had started to tighten the snowpack. Stabilization by howitzer fire commenced, and by late afternoon the avalanche cycle was over, and the highway once again was safe for travel.

When the Canadian Pacific Railway completed its line over Rogers Pass in 1885, the only known defences against avalanches were snowsheds. These sheds shielded the rails from avalanches in areas where snowslides were a known problem, but they were far from a foolproof method of defence. Particularly large avalanches could destroy the wooden structures, and they were constantly damaged by fire. Avalanches also could hit the line at points which had not been identified as trouble zones.

During the first century of railway operation through the park, more than 200 died in snowslides. On the night of 4 March 1910 an avalanche claimed 62 lives in a single stroke. This happened within sight of the location of the 1966 highway accident. It is to the credit of the modern highway avalanche control team, the park wardens and the park maintenance crews that there have been only two fatalities in twenty-five years of highway operation.

Static defences such as snowsheds, dams, dykes and trigger zone fences are now also used to protect certain areas of the highway. However, the modern system of mobile defence aims to stabilize accumulations of snow before they reach dangerous proportions.

THE NATURE OF AVALANCHES

No one knows how many avalanches come down each year in the backcountry of Mount Revelstoke and Glacier parks. Since more than 1500 avalanches affect the highway each winter, many times that number must break in the wilderness areas. Soil and vegetation studies show that at least 20 per cent of all park lands are directly influenced by avalanches.

Snowslides rank as one of the great powers of nature in these mountains. In Rogers Pass, the National Research Council has measured avalanche forces of 54 tonnes per square metre. To put this in perspective, 3 tonnes/m^2 is enough force to knock down a house and 10 tonnes/m^2 can rip a path through a mature evergreen forest.

Like all of the forces which carve our mountains, avalanches create as well as destroy. Although midwinter snowslides are usually snow moving over snow, in the spring it is common for the slides to break right to the ground and carry rocks and soil down slope. These wet spring slides occur when mild weather has brought the entire snowpack to the melting point and saturated it with water. The weakened snowpack ruptures and relatively slowly rumbles its way down the avalanche path, gouging the bottom and sides of the path and depositing the debris in its run-out zone. Like deltas at the mouth of a river, fans of material build up over the years at the toe of a snowslide and testify to the role of avalanches in shaping the mountain landscape.

Without the tree-clearing strength of snow avalanches, a continuous forest would cover a much larger area of these mountains. By cutting clear-

Wildflowers carpet avalanche slopes in May

ings, avalanches allow a diverse community of sun-loving plants and animals to live in the parks. An example is the slide alder which flourishes on open avalanche slopes. This supple-stemmed shrub bends easily under the weight of the snowpack and is rarely uprooted by the force of an avalanche.

Avalanche paths are important seasonal habitats for a number of birds and mammals. Shrub-loving birds such as Wilson's warblers and MacGillivray's warblers nest in the slidepath vegetation. Small rodents such as red-backed voles and deer mice abound in areas of moist slide alder.

On the steepest slopes of an avalanche path, snowslides often have removed much of the snowpack by early spring. Weeks before other areas in the mountains are snow free, these tracks melt out. Warm weather accelerates plant growth, and soon a hopeful green blanket covers the slopes. Waves of yellow avalanche lilies and white spring beauties adorn the paths while on either side, the forest is still buried by several metres of snow.

39

The greening vegetation found on these avalanche tracks provides a nutritious food source for several species of park mammals. By mid-May mountain goats have left their winter range cliffs to congregate on the areas of green-up. Bears, both grizzly and black, roam these paths grazing on the flowers and digging up the energy-packed roots of slidepath plants. Bears may also be attracted to the avalanche paths in spring by the carcasses of animals killed by snowslides, such as mountain goat, caribou, moose and wolverine.

THINGS TO SEE IN AVALANCHE COUNTRY

Whereas avalanches rate among the most spectacular natural phenomena in the Columbia Mountains, they are exceedingly dangerous to observe. At the times when you are likely to see one, the highway is usually closed. Furthermore, many come down at night and during periods of poor visibility. When avalanche danger has been identified, a strict no-stopping rule in the park further limits your likelihood of seeing a slide.

Although the Snow Research and Avalanche Warning Section is active all winter, you will rarely see its personnel. Most of their work takes them up into the elevations where avalanches are triggered. Even if you are stopped at a roadblock for avalanche control during the winter, the actual action will usually be out of sight.

Because of the difficulty in seeing avalanches, Environment Canada—Parks has sponsored a movie called *Snow War* which shows several snowslides in action. You can see the movie at any time in the Rogers Pass Information Centre. Displays in the centre further explain the nature and power of avalanches in the park.

If you travel through the Glacier park area during the winter or early spring, you are very likely to see snow piles from downed avalanches. When you pass through the snowsheds in Rogers Pass, avalanche snow may cover at least part of the shed roofs. In April and May, the dirty deposits of wet spring slides provide excellent subjects for photography.

At any time of the year, avalanche paths are clearly visible from the highway. The best viewing opportunities are in Glacier park where the higher elevation brings you closer to the slidepaths. During the snow-free months, the summit of Rogers Pass is an excellent place to view the active slopes of Macdonald West Shoulder. At Park One Picnic Area, near the west boundary of Glacier park, an interpretive display explains the role of avalanches in park ecology. A large pile of snow and avalanche debris usually persists throughout the summer here and makes it an excellent place to photograph an avalanche path.

To see the display of wildflowers which carpet avalanche paths, you should time your visit between mid-May and mid-June. You will be able to see the flowers where the highway crosses avalanche slopes. If you leave your car to explore these flower slopes, be sure to observe great caution, for the same flowers attract bears. Even though the slopes along the highway may be snow free, the higher regions of the avalanche path may be out of sight and still charged with snow. Warnings in the form of "no stopping" signs are placed at vulnerable viewpoints when this condition exists.

Near the western boundary of Glacier park you can see the results of an avalanche moving uphill. Stop at the snowsheds just outside the park and look at the slope across the valley to the west. Slides over the centre snowshed regularly cross the narrow valley and snap trees as they dissipate their force uphill.

Many trails in Glacier cross avalanche paths. Along the Asulkan Trail (p. 94) most of the upper valley is an active avalanche zone. On the Sir Donald Trail (p. 91), about 2 km from the trailhead, you can see numerous large trees uprooted by a powerful avalanche in 1972. Avalanches during other winters, such as 1985, have added to the debris. For short hikes through avalanche terrain, the Abandoned Rails Trail (p. 98) and Loop Trail (p. 89) offer walks of less than an hour that cross through bands of avalanche vegetation. On Loop Trail, a huge railway pillar toppled by a recent avalanche provides a graphic example of the power of snowslides.

Everyone travelling the Trans-Canada Highway passes through five concrete snowsheds shielding the highway on the eastern side of Rogers Pass. Another three snowsheds are located just west of the park on provincial lands. You also will see several circular concrete pads beside the highway used to position the howitzer during the winter. At Tractor Sheds Picnic Area, a viewpoint sign explains the aiming strategy used to align the cannon during avalanche stabilization shoots.

Relic snowsheds from the original days of the Canadian Pacific Railway can be seen in several places: Tractor Sheds Picnic Area, Abandoned Rails Trail and Loop Trail. On Abandoned Rails Trail, exhibits explain the several types of snowsheds used by the railway. The architecture of the Rogers Pass Centre was inspired by the design of the original CPR snowsheds.

Clockwise from top right: cinnamon-coloured black bear; Columbian ground squirrel; cariboo; hoary marmot; mountain goats

ANIMALS IN A VERTICAL WORLD

Mysterious footprints wove through the maze of crevasses that marked the Geikie Glacier icefall. From the avalanche-scarred valley of the Incomappleux River, an animal had gained the glacier, surmounted its major obstacle, and headed across the Illecillewaet Névé, a sea of ice cradled by the summits of the Sir Donald and Dawson ranges. Park naturalist Bob Brade and park wardens Greg Slatter and Roger Eddy were incredulous. The wildlife survey crew helicopter banked and followed the trail out onto the icefield. To that point, the 28 March 1985 game count had been routine.

TRACKING LARGE MAMMALS

Each March or early April park staff conduct aerial surveys in order to monitor long-term changes in large animal populations. This year, as usual, mountain goats had been the most abundant animal tallied. The shaggy white beasts are well adapted to rugged mountain terrain and by living on the cliffs, they avoid the deepest snows. At an estimated population of 300 for Glacier and 50 for Mount Revelstoke, they outnumber any other ungulate in the parks by more than ten to one.

Although the team had not seen any caribou that day, tracks had crossed the slopes in the headwaters of Mountain Creek. Supported on top of the snowpack by their huge hooves, a few caribou still wandered into Glacier National Park. In typical late winter fashion, the caribou had skirted the treeline and visited small clumps of subalpine fir. Old man's beard, a lichen rich in carbohydrates but poor in total nutritional value, draped the subalpine forests and provided the caribou with late winter survival food. Already they would be thin; by spring, ribs would corrugate their sides.

A hundred years ago, caribou had been a common sight in Glacier, but for reasons not completely understood, they had declined in numbers, and now any evidence of the animals using the park was of great interest. In

Mount Revelstoke these lichen-eaters appeared to be faring better; just the week before Brade had seen three, and bedding signs showed that about ten animals were living in the upper subalpine forests between Miller and Eva lakes.

In the lower reaches of Mountain Creek, the wildlife patrol also had spotted two moose. Although clouds had obscured the best moose habitat in the park—the Beaver River valley—ground surveys earlier in the season had indicated that about eight additional moose were wintering in Glacier. Very few moose live in either park. Excessively deep winter snow in most areas severely limits the winter range. Even in the Beaver valley, the moose range was marginal. In the recorded history of the parks, moose are newcomers, first appearing on game reports in 1930. Unless the climate takes a swing towards less snow, it is unlikely that many moose will ever be seen on these surveys.

Deep winter snow also makes life nearly impossible for elk, mule deer and white-tailed deer—and the survey team did not expect to see any on their March flight. Although a few elk and deer struggle through the winter on the lowest slopes of Mount Revelstoke and in the depths of the Beaver valley, most wildlife counts turn up none. In the snowfree months, a small number of elk and mule deer roam the high passes and avalanche paths on the east side of Glacier. White-tailed deer occasionally are spotted in the shrubby lowlands flanking Mount Revelstoke and the Beaver River.

Unlike the deer, bears thrive in this snow country. Most den in October and emerge in late March and April to feast on winter-killed animals and the first harvests of wildflowers. In fact, the combination of heavy snow-fall and steep terrain found in both parks causes numerous avalanches which open up the forests to produce favoured feeding grounds for both grizzlies and blacks. Flowers and shrubs abound in these avalanche scars, and slidepath greenery and berries provide the bears with the majority of their food. Despite appearances and reputation, these large carnivores are primarily vegetarians in this area. They will not pass up the chance to scavenge an occasional carcass, and will eat almost any small animal, bird or insect that comes within reach, but their main diet is salad.

Although it was early in the season for bears, the survey crew had hoped to see a few tracks on the snow. Already, just north of Mount Revelstoke, a radio-collared grizzly, nicknamed Ace by the British Columbia Wildlife Branch, had dug himself out of his high elevation den. And near the west boundary of the park, several black bears had left their winter homes in hollow cedar trees and been spotted by motorists on the Trans-Canada Highway. But in Glacier, there was no sign of bear activity; the bears were still resting in their dens.

Large mammals such as bears attract much interest, but they actually ac-count for only 20 per cent of the fifty-three mammal species recorded in the parks. Both in terms of diversity and abundance, lesser mammals make up most of park wildlife. Medium-sized animals, the size of a lynx or coyote, account for 15 per cent of the list, and the remaining species are small mammals such as shrews, bats, mice and weasels. Although the game survey team spotted the far-ranging tracks of a wolverine on their March flight, aerial counts rarely reveal the presence of medium and small mammals.

In adaptation to the stresses of cold and snow, smaller mammals survive the winter in a variety of ways. Some, like the familiar Columbian ground squirrel, hibernate. Others, such as the mice and voles, and their predators, the shrews and weasels, live in tunnels beneath the snowpack. Oversized feet support snowshoe hares and lynx on the surface of the snow. Bats simply avoid the winter by flying away from the parks—though no one knows exactly where they go.

*   *   *

Perhaps distracted by the noise of the helicopter, the jet black wolf stopped and surveyed the aircraft. With seeming indifference it watched as the machine circled overhead. Inside the helicopter, the naturalist and wardens babbled in excitement. Following the tracks had resulted in the park's second verified sighting of a timber wolf. Not only was this a rare observation but it also suggested a wolf with mountaineering ability more befitting a mountain goat. As the helicopter circled again, the animal turned and continued its transglacial trot, its itinerary forever a mystery.

BIRDS

Unlike the mammals, few birds reside in Mount Revelstoke and Glacier parks the year round. The majority, such as warblers, vireos and flycatchers, only visit the parks during the warmest months of the year—a time when a superabundance of insect life provides them with a rich source of food. They come here to nest and when their young are reared, they return to their tropical homes.

Red-eyed vireos provide a good example of a neotropical migrant's way of life. After a month's journey from Venezuela, they arrive in the parks in late May. During the long days of June they establish breeding territories in the shrubby forests. Within ten weeks they have built nests, hatched four eggs, fledged young, and are on their way south. Although many die on the return journey to South America, especially the young of the year, the advantage of an abundant food supply outweighs the perils of migration. On the balance sheet, red-eyed vireos spend about half the year in the tropics, a quarter of the year in transit and a quarter in the parks.

Of the 235 species of birds known in the parks' region, only about 30 have found ways to overcome the lean months of winter and can be found

MIKE PIRNKE

MIKE PIRNKE

*Rufous hummingbirds spend only a few
months in the parks*

Steller's jays live here year-round

here during any month of the year. The best-known residents include common ravens, Steller's jays, gray jays, four species of chickadees, four species of grouse, most woodpeckers and owls, and golden-crowned kinglets.

American dippers live along cascades at all elevations in Mount Revelstoke and Glacier parks. These amazing songbirds feed in rushing mountain streams. Using their wings as propellers, they fly under the water in search of aquatic invertebrates. The sight of a small bird diving into a summer torrent is impressive, but it is even more so in winter when, seemingly oblivious to the temperature, dippers continue their cold-defying life-style. As if to boast of their hardiness, they sing throughout the short days of winter.

While most species of birds have well-established routines of coming and going, one group, the "winter" finches, is unpredictable. Some years pine siskins, red crossbills and white-winged crossbills invade the mountains in late autumn. Feeding on abundant crops of tree seeds, many remain to breed during the winter, spring or early summer. After nesting, a few may stay on—or they may vanish entirely.

In late November 1984, for example, hundreds of thousands of siskins moved into the area of the parks. It was not unusual to see a single flock of a thousand or more, and hundreds were killed daily on the highway. The following April the big flocks dispersed, and siskins set up breeding colonies in the dense coniferous forests. Until mid-June, you could see or hear a siskin almost anywhere. Then, with the first days of summer, they vanished. Nor did they return that autumn. Forests which had teemed with

Northern alligator lizard

life one winter were completely silent the next. In the decade from 1975 to 1985 siskin invasions followed by a total exodus have been observed twice in Mount Revelstoke and Glacier parks.

Where do these gypsy birds come from? And where do they go? There is very little evidence, but one bird killed on the highway in the spring of 1984 in Mount Revelstoke had been banded two winters earlier at Whiting, New Jersey, 3500 km away near the Atlantic coast!

NORTHERN LIZARDS AND OTHER COLD-BLOODED MOUNTAINEERS

For a warm-blooded animal such as a bird or a mammal, the cold and snowy climate of the Columbia Mountains presents a formidable challenge. For a slow-moving reptile or amphibian, invasion of these mountains is nearly impossible. In fact, only three reptiles and four amphibians have gained toeholds in Mount Revelstoke and Glacier national parks. In a decade of careful searching, one experienced park biologist has observed snakes on only three occasions. The two species of garter snakes found here are completely harmless and among the parks' rarest animals.

Although the word lizard is synonymous with dry, hot terrain, the northern alligator lizard lives in Mount Revelstoke at the northern extremity of its known range in North America. If you search carefully, you can find one of these hardy creatures almost any summer day.

Park amphibians include a single salamander, a toad and two frogs. Although none is abundant, the western toad is the most widespread. Breeding aggregations can be found in the Beaver River valley as early as April, and some still will be mating in early August at the summit of Mount Revelstoke. A tough species, they have been observed at 2000 m elevation at the summit of Jade Lakes Pass.

BUTTERFLIES, GLACIER CRAWLERS AND OTHER CRITTERS

No one knows how many invertebrates live in the parks. One estimate puts the number in the 25 000 species range. Two groups, the butterflies and an ecological assemblage of "snow insects," are the best known.

Sixty-five species of butterflies have been found in Mount Revelstoke and Glacier parks. According to a detailed study conducted in the late 1970s, butterflies can be seen from early spring to autumn, and from the lowest park forests to the windswept summits. Most are permanent residents in the parks and persist during the winter as either eggs or hibernating adults. One species, the painted lady, seems to have a life-style similar to the pine siskin: some years it is here in unexpected abundance; then, after a mass outbound migration in September, it may not be seen again for several years.

Unlike the majority of invertebrates, snow insects are at home in subzero winter temperatures. This highly specialized group of unrelated animals is active throughout the winter months during which they complete important phases of their life cycles. For example, wingless craneflies walk across the snow surface in search of mates on days when temperatures are in the range of 0° C to -4° C. When they encounter members of the opposite sex, they join and continue their march in a twelve-legged dance. Bizarre-shaped, flightless scorpionflies also mate on the winter snow surface; like the snow craneflies, they retreat beneath the snowpack if the temperature gets either too warm or too cold for their comfort. There is even a tiny midge which has been observed performing its aerial mating dance over the Illecillewaet River during a December snowstorm.

This winter microcosm even supports special predators: snow spiders and glacier crawlers, insects so rare that they have their own order. Apparently feasting on other snow invertebrates, these unlikely winter animals are a marvel of life's adaptability.

FISH

In 1888 an adventurous explorer tried fishing in Marion Lake and later wrote ". . . I incline to the belief that the reason why the fish did not rise was because there were none there." He had discovered a basic fact about park waters: they are either barren or contain few fish.

Although the Columbia River embracing the parks has a varied fish life, only six types of fish have invaded park waters: rainbow trout, cutthroat trout, Dolly Varden (bull-trout), long-nosed sucker, slimy sculpin and mountain whitefish. An additional species, the eastern brook trout, has been successfully introduced.

Barriers such as waterfalls and cascades prevent fish from naturally establishing in the alpine zone, but over the years stocking programs have resulted in self-sustaining populations in a few waters. This artificial manipulation of park wildlife is now viewed as unacceptable, and stocking has ceased.

OBSERVING WILDLIFE

The monthly calendars on pp. 103–21 provide suggestions for seasonal wildlife viewing. In general, you will see more animals if you drive or hike either very early or late in the day. Do not expect birds and mammals to be active during a hot August afternoon when the highway is clogged with traffic.

Bear: Mid-May through early June is the best time to view bears in the parks. They are just out of hibernation and often can be seen from the highway. Scan the avalanche slopes in Rogers Pass for both grizzlies and blacks. When the dandelions bloom, black bears often consume a floral salad at roadside. During July and August bears are harder to spot because of the dense vegetation. Try an early morning drive along the Trans-Canada keeping a sharp lookout for blacks. By this time, grizzlies have usually moved up slope into the upper subalpine/alpine tundra. Do not be surprised to see a ''cinnamon'' bear; about 10 per cent of our black bears are actually brown in colour. Treat all bears with great respect.

Mountain Goat: Goats may be seen all year above the highway snowsheds on the eastern side of Rogers Pass. From the Tractor Sheds picnic area just east of the Rogers Pass Information Centre, look for off-white forms near rocky areas. (Binoculars are recommended.) Many visitors to the parks mistake our mountain goats for sheep. Bighorn sheep are brown and white and are not found in these mountains because there is no suitable winter range.

Beaver and muskrat: Both species are common along Skunk Cabbage Trail in Mount Revelstoke and in the Beaver River valley in Glacier.

Birdwatching: May and June are the best months. Birdwatching hot spots include Skunk Cabbage Trail, the base of the Summit Road (both in Mount Revelstoke) and the Beaver River valley (Glacier). A drive up Mount Revelstoke's Summit Road in early July will often reveal species characteristic of the major life zones. Park interpreters can provide you with topical information on birdwatching and would be happy to make note of your observations. Detailed lists of park animals are available from the staff.

RAINFOREST, SNOWFOREST, NO FOREST

T wo hundred metres west of Giant Cedars Picnic Area, Mount Revelstoke, 1 April 1966—With the force of a tornado, a storm brushed against the mountainside. Huge western red cedars, survivors of a millennium, bent with the wind, and then lost their grip on the gravelly soil. Before the storm veered away from the valley wall, a patch of forest the size of a baseball field was levelled, and the dark understory beneath the trees became a sunny nursery for new growth. Weather, the master gardener of the mountains, had opened the old forest, and in a year or two, MacGillivray's warblers would have shrubby song perches in the valley.

THE NEW FORESTS

When you walk among trees that measure generations by the century, it is easy to feel dwarfed by time. The forests of Mount Revelstoke and Glacier, ancient by our standards, are recent invaders when compared to the mountains. Ice sheets obliterated life from this area of British Columbia for much of the past million years during the last great age of glaciation. All the plants we see here today have recolonized the Columbias during the past ten to fifteen thousand years—an instant in the 185-million-year history of these mountains.

In this moment of geological time, mosaics of tundra and forest invaded the once-barren valleys. Gravels washed by frigid meltwaters became flower beds, then shrubby meadows, and finally forests. Guided by the hand of climate, a rainforest of huge trees now dominates the mild, wet valleys. Higher, where snow deepens and temperatures drop, subalpine forests cover the slopes. Nearing the peaks, extremes of wind and cold bring a final halt to the trees, and meadows of heath and sedge creep to the edge of the remaining glaciers. Higher still, where rock meets the sky, lichens encrust the ridges at the limits of life.

In response to the differences in climates from valley to summit, vegetation has painted the mountains with a variety hard to equal anywhere else

---

Kindergarten class rings a western red cedar   JOHN G. WOODS in Canada. Here, at a glance, your eye can journey across zones of climate and vegetation comparable to a trip from Toronto to Baffin Island.

PATTERNS IN THE SKY

Ecologists working in Mount Revelstoke and Glacier national parks recognize four major life zones: cedar-hemlock forest (also called interior rainforest or Columbia forest), lower subalpine forest, upper subalpine forest and alpine tundra.

At the lowest elevations, from about 500 m to 1500 m, the cedar-hemlock zone gives park visitors a taste of the type of rainforest also found along the Pacific coast. Mild temperatures and abundant moisture support forests of western red cedar and western hemlock. Beneath the trees lies a verdant mat of lady fern and oak fern. Where shafts of sunlight pierce the gloom, dense thickets of devil's club and occasional clumps of Pacific yew congest the understory. Wrinkled patches of lungwort lichen cling to the trees, and feather mosses blanket the old trunks that litter the forest floor.

While this pattern of old rainforest broadly characterizes the cedar-hemlock belt and makes it obviously distinct from other zones, ecologists have further divided these low elevation forests into nineteen "ecosites" based on the finer designs of plant species, soil, bedrock and landform. For example, the ancient rainforest at Giant Cedars Trail in Mount Revelstoke park is classified as the Lauretta 1 ecosite—LR1 in the scientist's codebook. A short distance down the highway at Skunk Cabbage Picnic Area, the area is mapped as a Griffith 1 (GF1) ecosite—still part of the cedar-hemlock zone, but this time a site featuring waterlogged soils with scattered hemlock and cedar and a swampy understory of skunk cabbage, horsetail, sedge, alder and cottonwood. A few kilometres farther west, above the western boundary of Mount Revelstoke, another ecosite, Nordic 6 (NC6), illustrates the driest extreme of the cedar-hemlock forest. NC6 is an open forest of western white pine and trembling aspen growing on a thin, rocky soil with an understory of mountain box. When plotted on park maps, these ecosites produce a patchwork reflecting the complexity in climate, geology, soil and vegetation found in the Columbia Mountains.

Moving up slope, at about 1500 m colder temperatures and greater snowfall dictate a dramatic shift to another life zone. Here, a closed forest of spirelike Engelmann spruce, subalpine fir and mountain hemlock define the lower subalpine forest. These are the lichen forests of the Columbias where dark draperies of old man's beard lichen swing pendants along the tree branches. Below, ferns give way to white rhododendron and black huckleberry.

With increasing elevation, snowfall also increases. By about 1900 m elevation, the deep snowpacks are often twice the height of a man and may not melt completely until late July. In this upper subalpine zone, scattered

Snow-encrusted subalpine trees

groves of spruce and subalpine fir line the edges of natural flower meadows. Here, in a brief rush to complete their life cycle, wildflowers such as glacier lily, spring beauty, mountain valerian, lupine, mountain spiraea and heather put on an outstanding but brief show of colour in late July and early August. Complexities within both subalpine zones add another twenty-five ecosites to the ecological inventory.

Above 2200 m elevation, areas of the treeless alpine zone appear like islands in a sea of forested valleys—outposts for plant life in the parks. Severe cold and wind rule this zone for much of the year, and normal tree life cannot survive. Many of the wildflowers found in the subalpine meadows reach the alpine but rarely put on an overpowering display. In some areas, the ground is simply barren.

The ecological inventory of the alpine zone lists six ecosites plus a variety of miscellaneous landscapes such as glaciers, recent moraines and rocklands. Even here, a few plants manage to persist—isolated clumps of purple saxifrage growing on a high summit, a clump of holly fern hidden in the shelter of a boulder, or a profusion of snow algae tinting the persistent snowfields red.

VIEWING PARK FORESTS AND WILDFLOWERS

Although early botanists occasionally remarked at the lack of diversity of plant life in these parks, recent studies show that they were mistaken. In fact, the impressive statistics shown by the current tally include 546 species of flowering plants, about a sixth of the known flora of the entire province. With an additional 36 liverworts, 130 mosses, 129 lichens and an estimated 1000 species of mushrooms, you could spend a lifetime learning to identify plants here.

Algae can turn snow patches red in summer

Skunk cabbage blooms in April   *Indian paintbrush blooms in August*

A good way to get an overview of park vegetation zones is to drive up the Summit Road in Mount Revelstoke National Park. This 26-km gravel road is usually open to the summit from late July to late September. On this short drive you will pass through the cedar-hemlock, lower subalpine and upper subalpine zones. From the summit you can see the extensive alpine tundra zone, and you can hike the Jade Lakes Trail (pp. 84–85) into this land above the trees. In early August the subalpine meadows put on their famous display of colour.

Several nature trails in Mount Revelstoke park are designed to introduce park flora. Giant Cedars and Skunk Cabbage trails (pp. 86,87) guide you through two ecosites of the cedar-hemlock zone; Mountain Meadows Trail (p. 85) explores the ecology of the upper subalpine. The sections entitled Hiking Trails (pp. 81–101) and A Columbia Mountains Calendar (pp. 103–121) suggest places and times to see park vegetation at its most representative.

STEEL RAILS, CARIBOU TRAILS

In the spring of 1881 a small party of trail-worn explorers struggled their way up the Illecillewaet River valley and into the heart of the territory now encompassing Glacier National Park. Railway pathfinder Maj. Albert Bowman Rogers, his nephew Albert and their native porters overcame the obstacles that had barred others and on 29 May discovered the key to the Selkirks—the narrow pass between the peaks and glaciers which would be named for its discoverer and soon carry the main line of Canada's first transcontinental railway.

"Such a view! Never to be forgotten!" Albert later wrote. "Our eyesight caromed from one bold peak to another for miles in all directions. The wind blew fiercely across the ridge and scuddy clouds were whirled in the eddies behind great towering peaks of bare rocks. Everything was covered in a shroud of white, giving the whole landscape the appearance of snow-clad desolation . . . the grandeur of the view, sublime beyond conception, crowded out all thought of our discomforts."

Within five years of this momentous discovery, the Canadian Pacific Railway was operating its main line through Rogers Pass, and the surrounding lands had been set aside as a national park reserve. In the century that followed, the pass became internationally known as an exciting route for travellers on both the railway and the Trans-Canada Highway. And with this access into the wilderness, Albert's praise for the mountain scenery would be echoed time and again by visitors to Glacier National Park, and her sister park, Mount Revelstoke.

FIRST FOOTSTEPS
The extremely rugged terrain of the northern Columbia Mountains, their harsh climate and impassable snows make of the region a no-man's-land. In fact, archaeologists have not yet been able to establish that native peoples ever lived in the areas covered by the parks. While Indians tra-

Snowshed construction along the original CPR *line in Rogers Pass*

velled and camped along the Columbia River, there was little to attract them into the snowy mountains with their awesome avalanches and poor hunting. Undoubtedly there was some travel through Rogers Pass, up the major valleys and onto the summit of Mount Revelstoke, but Indian use seems to have been infrequent.

Our history of the north Columbias starts with the travels of European explorers in their efforts to map the West. In the early years of the nineteenth century, mapmaker David Thompson used the Columbia River as his highway but avoided the mountains. By midcentury, prospectors were not only travelling the river but also probing the heights for precious minerals. Using trails worn deep by generations of caribou and mountain goat, they penetrated the secret places of the Selkirks and Purcells and occasionally found gold, silver and copper. They may have even crossed the mountains by way of the long-sought passes, but if they did, they left no record of their discoveries. It was not until Canada embarked on its construction of a transcontinental railway that serious exploration of these mountains took place.

Unlike the Rocky Mountains, where Indians led European explorers through mountain passes already familiar to them, the North Columbia long remained a barrier to east-west travel. In 1865 surveyor Walter

Moberly partially solved the problem when he discovered Eagle Pass—the route now connecting Revelstoke and Sicamous. But he was thwarted by the Selkirks, and although his expedition penetrated up the Illecillewaet to within 30 km of Rogers Pass, it fell short of establishing a route for the railway.

For nearly a generation the Selkirks were once again shunned as the railway sought a route through the Yellowhead Pass—the present area of Jasper National Park. However, once the firm decision was made to build a more southern rail line up the Bow River valley from Calgary, attention again focussed on the Selkirk blockade. When the fifty-two-year-old Major Rogers finally pushed his men to the summit of the Selkirks in 1881, the railway and the country were elated—the seemingly impenetrable Selkirks had been conquered.

THE RAILWAY

Today the speed with which railway construction through Rogers Pass took place seems amazing—the pass was discovered in 1881, surveyed in 1882–83 and the line completed in 1885. Defying obstacles of dense forest, flooding rivers, steep grades and snow avalanches, the builders laid their twin bands of steel through country that fought them every step of the way. When the line was finished in the autumn of 1885, winter halted operations. In 1886 the numerous snowsheds were built, and the Canadian Pacific Railway commenced "normal" service to the coast. In those days, regular winter operations included an ongoing battle with deep snows and avalanches which often closed the line for weeks at a time. These conditions also led to a constantly growing list of fatalities—over 200 railway men lost their lives beneath Albert's "shroud of white."

By 1912 the railway had had enough of Rogers Pass—its steep approaches up the Beaver River valley, its gauntlet of avalanche paths and its gloomy, fire-prone snowsheds. They laid plans for an underground assault on the mountains. A tunnel 8 km long beneath Mount Macdonald would not only avoid the worst avalanches but also reduce much of the grade. Again with feverish speed, the railway got on with the job and in 1916 opened the Connaught Tunnel.

Nearly three generations of railway men operated this line through the Beaver and Illecillewaet valleys and beneath Rogers Pass, constantly adjusting its line, improving the bridges and working on the few remaining snowsheds, until progress dictated another assault on the mountains.

With increasingly heavy trains and mounting traffic, the steep approach up the Beaver valley into Connaught Tunnel had become a bottleneck on the line. Six extra locomotives were needed to push the heavy modern trains up to the tunnel entrance; obviously the railway was fast approaching its maximum capacity. Once again, tunnelling was seen as the answer. The complex scheme included twinning the line through Glacier, a new, more gentle grade up the Beaver, an elaborate ventilation system and two new tunnels, the 1.8-km Mount Shaughnessy Tunnel and the 14.7-km Mount Macdonald Tunnel under Rogers Pass.

In 1984 CP Rail started on this project, which was second in magnitude only to the original construction of the railway a century earlier. Using mining techniques of blast and haul from the west and a giant laser-guided tunnel-boring machine from the east, the company again pitched battle with the mountains men like to describe in superlatives.

GLACIER'S NEW MOUNTAINEERS

With the railway came an explosion of interest in touring the north Columbia Mountains. The CPR had foreseen the tourist appeal of the area and supported the establishment of Glacier National Park. They even ran a special summer track outside some of the wooden avalanche sheds so that tourists could enjoy the spectacular glacier scenery. At the first crossing of the Illecillewaet River, the CPR built a hotel, Glacier House, which soon became the hub of tourism and exploration in this part of British Columbia.

The year 1888 was pivotal in the history of both Glacier park and the sport of mountaineering. That year two members of the British Alpine Club stayed at Glacier House and made several landmark ascents in the pass area. Their crowning achievement was an ambitious climb to the summit of Mount Bonney at the headwaters of Loop Brook. Impressed by the potential for sport mountaineering in the Selkirks, one member of the team, Rev. William Spotswood Green, compiled a book of their adventures. Published in 1890, his classic account, *Among the Selkirk Glaciers,* inspired climbers from around the world to visit Glacier House and challenge the mountains. The firm quartzite rock and numerous glaciers appealed to climbers with experience in the similar terrain of the European Alps. Many historians credit this early activity as the origin of serious mountaineering in North America and consider Glacier park the birthplace of the sport.

Again in its dual role of railway company and tourism promoter, the CPR put Glacier on the map in 1899 by providing the services of trained Swiss guides for their guests at Glacier House. For a fee, even novice climbers could attempt the peaks under the experienced guidance of a qualified mountaineer.

For three decades following the discovery of Rogers Pass, mountaineering enjoyed its heyday in Glacier National Park. Record books and mountain-top cairns—the so-called "stonemen" of the peaks—chronicle a pageant of expeditions and landmarks.

In recognition of the attention which Glacier was attracting, the Geological Survey of Canada commissioned a detailed survey of the area in 1901

Visitors to Mount Revelstoke park, circa 1920

and 1902. Under the leadership of Arthur O. Wheeler, cartographer and skillful mountaineer, the survey team braved rivers, fought devil's club and scaled peaks around the pass. Wheeler's comprehensive report and accurate maps were made available to the public in 1905, and to this day they remain a vital source of information and perspective on the park.

"Owing to the great influx to our Canadian Alps, from all parts of the world, of those interested in mountain scenery, the subject has become one of great interest," wrote Wheeler in describing the reasons for the survey. His instructions directed him to survey the Selkirks adjacent to the CPR and pay most attention to the summit of Rogers Pass visited by tourists and mountain climbers during the summer months. Wheeler noted, "I refer to the inflow of tourists, globe-trotters, hunters, sight-seers and bona-fide mountain-climbers made possible by the construction of the railway."

In 1904 a discovery just west of Rogers Pass at the midpoint of the Cougar Brook valley added yet another attraction to the park. That year, Charles H. Deutschmann found a significant cave system in an unusually thick bed of pure limestone. Shortly after, Deutschmann was hired by the government to improve access within the caves and to guide tourists through the strange underground world. These tours of Nakimu Caves

ROGERS PASS ARCHIVES

Heather Lake Lodge

lasted until the mid-1930s when the declining fortunes of tourism and a poor national economy brought them to an end.

Following the opening of the Connaught Tunnel in 1916, tourism began a steady decline in Glacier. With the track in front of Glacier House abandoned, tourists could no longer stop there for lunch and had to be ferried up to the hotel from Glacier Station. By 1925 the expectation of poor profits and the constant threat of fire led the CPR to close Glacier House. The buildings were demolished in 1929.

For almost forty years, the park saw few visitors, although the Alpine

Club of Canada kept interest in the area alive by sponsoring several summer and winter camps in the pass. The old hotel grounds served as their camping grounds and the trails from the hotel as their access to the peaks. In 1962, when the Trans-Canada Highway opened over Rogers Pass, the peaks again became easily accessible, and a new era of mountaineering and tourism began in the park.

MOUNT REVELSTOKE

While Glacier enjoyed international fame during its early years, the scenic attractions of Mount Revelstoke remained largely unknown except to local residents. In an effort to change this, a group of citizens from the City of Revelstoke began to promote trips to the impressive alpine wildflower meadows at the summit of Mount Revelstoke, publicizing the area through photographic displays, articles in newspapers and letters to influential people. In 1914 they succeeded in having the mountain and adjacent drainages to the east declared a national park.

For many years Mount Revelstoke's national historic significance centred on the development of skiing. Revelstoke became one of the first areas on the continent where skiing was a popular sport, and trips up Mount Revelstoke were a traditional winter activity. For several years a downhill ski course and internationally ranked ski jump were located on the lower slopes of the mountain. Ski jumping championships gave Mount Revelstoke an international flavour comparable to that enjoyed by her sister park to the east.

Access to the summit was fundamental to the realization of a tourist industry in Mount Revelstoke, and work began on the Summit Road in 1911. By 1927 it had reached the summit at Heather Lake, and nine years later a lodge and tea house facility provided a "civilized" focal point for visitors enjoying the alpine scenery. Heather Lake Lodge was a much loved location, especially popular with photographers, but sadly for both residents and visitors it succumbed to economic pressures, and the buildings were dismantled in 1966. Today, thousands of visitors from around the world can easily drive to the summit of Mount Revelstoke and enjoy the superb wildflower meadows and pleasing alpine scenery.

THE TRANS-CANADA HIGHWAY

In 1962, three-quarters of a century after the railway first struggled across Rogers Pass, the narrow defile again became the focus for a massive construction project—the completion of the Trans-Canada Highway. With the advantage of detailed knowledge of climate and avalanche activity gained during the railway's history in the Selkirks, and advances in modern highway engineering, the federal government tackled the pass that had defeated the CPR years before.

Avalanches remained the chief problem for the highway builders, and the new roadway received careful study by international experts in the field of avalanche control and safety. Their solution to the problem was a dual approach—a mobile avalanche control program and a series of stationary defences placed in strategic locations. While the avalanche program draws most attention, other aspects of the highway operation present constant challenges. An average of 10 m of snowfall must be plowed from the steep grades in Rogers Pass each winter.

Bridging the numerous cascades along the highway and containing the capricious flows of mountain rivers has proven to be another major concern for maintenance of the highway through Mount Revelstoke and Glacier parks. In a prophetic observation made at the turn of the century, H. B. Muckleston, then Assistant Engineer, Pacific Divison, Canadian Pacific Railway, noted that ". . . the character of a mountain stream cannot be judged by a casual acquaintance; it has been found, by dear experience, that no mountain rivulet can be trusted to remain one for long." Serious flooding in July 1983 proved the accuracy of Muckleston's words when the highway was breached for ten days by the rampaging waters of Woolsey Creek. Damage to the railway at the same time illustrated that the natural forces operating in these mountains still dominate man's relationship to the land.

HISTORICAL PLACES TO VISIT

In Rogers Pass there are numerous ruins of the original railway line across the mountains. You can see old snowsheds and bridges, and walk portions of the right-of-way. Your explorations might best start at the Rogers Pass Information Centre, a building featuring railway history and located on the site of the second railway station in Rogers Pass. From the Centre, a short hike on Abandoned Rails Trail (p. 98) will reveal several old snowsheds and the site where sixty-two men were killed by a single avalanche in 1910. Other points of interest in the pass area include the Glacier House site, Loop Trail (p. 89), and several old bridges. Ask for the free publication *Snow War* in the Centre which contains a detailed guide to the history of Rogers Pass.

In Mount Revelstoke, the historic drive to the summit features viewpoints along the way marking points of natural and historical interest. At the summit, you can visit a fire tower built in 1928. The parking lot serves as trailhead for a number of excellent hiking trails.

A ROGERS PASS REFERENCE

Place Name	Significance
Fleming Peak	Sir Sandford Fleming, Chief Engineer for the CPR from its inception to 1881; crossed Rogers Pass in 1883 and wrote a vivid account of the journey
Mount Abbott	Henry Abbott an official of the CPR during the railway's construction years
Mount Macdonald	Sir John A. Macdonald, first Prime Minister of Canada (1867–73, 1878–91) and prime advocate of the need for a transcontinental railway
Mount Rogers	Major Albert Bowman Rogers, nicknamed ''The Railway Pathfinder,'' discovered Rogers Pass on 29 May 1881 while employed with the CPR
Mount Sifton	The Honourable Clifford Sifton, former Minister of the Interior
Mount Sir Donald	Sir Donald A. Smith, director of the CPR and the person who drove the last spike in the railway at Craigellachie, 7 November 1885
Mount Tupper	Sir Charles Tupper, a father of Confederation and officer of the CPR during the construction years

VISITING GLACIER COUNTRY

Although the extremely rugged mountains in Mount Revelstoke and Glacier national parks present obvious opportunities for the experienced mountaineer, other less strenuous activities are also to be enjoyed here. You can take a stroll on a nature trail, backpack along an alpine ridge or simply enjoy superb views from a roadside pull-off. A comprehensive interpretation program offers detailed information on the two parks including the special features of the Columbia Mountains.

The following suggestions for your visit are based on the combined experience of hundreds of park employees who have worked in Mount Revelstoke and Glacier over the years. Park staff will be happy to answer any of your questions.

HIKING, WALKING, BACKPACKING

The best way to get to know the parks is on foot. A network of twenty-six trails in Glacier and Mount Revelstoke parks takes you through all major life zones. The trails range in difficulty from ten-minute walks to strenuous, all-day climbs. Individual trail descriptions begin on p. 81.

Many people who enjoy a hiking holiday camp in Glacier park's Illecillewaet Campground. Numerous trails lead from this centrally located camping area. Most years, August is the best hiking month in both parks. Biting insects are rarely a serious problem in this area, but it is advisable to carry insect repellent just in case.

The difficult terrain found in both parks limits backpacking opportunities. However, Copperstain and Bostock trails in Glacier park and Jade Lakes Trail in Mount Revelstoke park are suitable for backcountry trips lasting a few days, and all three offer outstanding scenery. No camping is allowed within 3 km of the parks' roadways except in organized campgrounds. Registration is required for all overnight hiking and mountain climbing trips. Registration points for this public safety service are the

Glacier warden office and the park office in the city of Revelstoke.

Experienced members of the Park Interpretation staff usually schedule a series of conducted hikes in Glacier park each July and August. For groups of fifteen or more, the parks may be able to arrange a special conducted nature tour, a service available year-round. Contact the park well in advance to check on yearly schedules and staff availablility.

Hikers should be prepared for sudden changes in weather in the Columbia Mountains. Even in the hottest August weather experienced hikers carry spare sweaters and rain gear in their day packs. Carefully note the elevation range for each trail. Many trails above 1900 m are snow free only during August and September. A trail condition report is posted at all information outlets throughout the summer, or phone the park for up-to-date information.

Bears, both grizzly and black, are of special concern when hiking in wilderness country. If bears are considered to be a problem on particular trails, these trails will be closed, but hikers must remain alert on all trails. Pets may provoke confrontations with bears and other wildlife. For your own (and your pet's) safety, protection of wildlife and the enjoyment of others, keep pets under close physical control, or leave them at home. Publications and advice on hiking in bear country are available at all park offices and from visitor services staff, park interpreters and wardens.

When hiking in Glacier, you may find unexploded howitzer shells from winter avalanche control operations. If you come upon a strange metal object, don't touch it—it could explode. Report its presence immediately to the nearest park office.

TRAIL SUGGESTIONS

Glacier views—Abbott Ridge, Glacier Crest, Avalanche Crest
Wildflowers—Mountain Meadows, Balu Pass, Skunk Cabbage
Birdwatching—Skunk Cabbage, Loop
Alpine hiking—Copperstain, Bostock, Jade Lakes
Short strolls—Meeting of the Waters, Giant Cedars, Inspiration Woods
Historic walks—Abandoned Rails, Loop
Backpacking—Copperstain, Bostock, Jade Lakes

GLACIER TRAVEL, MOUNTAIN CLIMBING

Glacier travel and mountain climbing are potentially hazardous activities requiring skill and experience. Those who wish to take mountaineering trips in the parks must register at the Glacier warden office or the Revelstoke park office. Several private mountain guides are licensed to take the public on mountaineering expeditions in the parks. Contact any park office for a list of guides offering these commercial services.

Glacier park has been an important sport centre for climbing since the late 1880s. The Alpine Club of Canada has had a long association with the park and owns and operates the Wheeler Hut at Illecillewaet Campground. Permission to use this private cabin must be obtained in advance from the club. Contact the ACC, Box 1026, Banff, Alberta TOL OCO (403/762-4481), for information on the hut and organized mountaineering expeditions in the park.

The city of Revelstoke and the town of Golden both have departments that organize mountaineering activities in the national parks. For information contact City of Revelstoke, Parks and Recreation Department, Box 170, 600 Campbell Avenue, Revelstoke, B.C. VOE 2SO (604/837-9351) or Town of Golden, Parks and Recreation Department, Box 350, 916 – 9th Avenue East, Golden, B.C. VOA 1HO (604/344-2271).

Backcountry cabins are available courtesy of the national parks for use by mountaineers at Eva Lake, Glacier Circle and Sapphire Col. A climbing guide covering Mount Revelstoke and Glacier parks is listed in the Suggested Reading section of this book (see William L. Putnam, p. 124). Detailed route photographs of popular climbs can be viewed at the park warden office in Rogers Pass.

CAVE EXPLORATION

All caves in national parks are closed to the general public. Nakimu Caves in Glacier park contain both dangerous passageways and delicate formations which make strict control necessary. The caves are gated to ensure that this regulation is observed.

Special permits authorizing cave visits may be issued by the Park Superintendent; however, these permits are restricted to groups with demonstrated caving expertise such as caving clubs and scientists. Applications for access into Nakimu should be made by an authorized person in writing and addressed to the Park Superintendent.

Caving clubs welcome new members and provide training in caving (also known as spelunking). For more information contact the Vancouver Island Cave Explorations Group, 234 Edward Street, Victoria, B.C. V9A 3E5 (604/386-6250). They will be happy to answer your questions and direct you to the nearest cave exploration club in western North America.

HORSEBACK RIDING

Horseback riding is not permitted on Mount Revelstoke trails. In Glacier you can ride on the Beaver, Bostock, Copperstain and Flat Creek trails, but riders must obtain a grazing permit at the Glacier warden office before heading out on an overnight trip. Park wardens use horses on these trails and can provide up-to-date information on trail conditions. No commercial riding is available in the park although guided trail rides are offered in the Golden and Revelstoke areas.

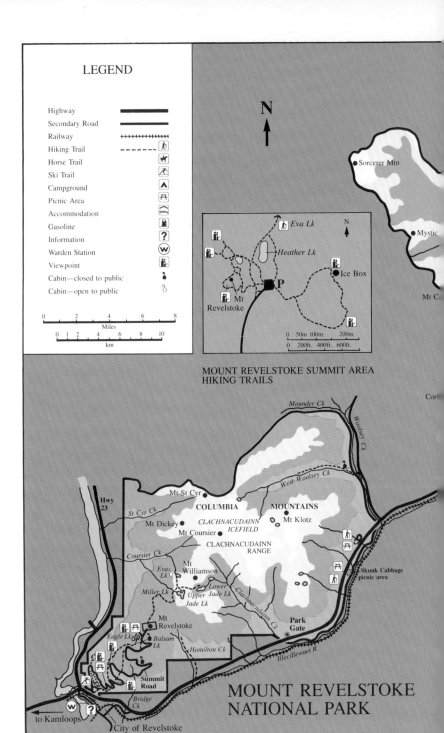

LEGEND

Highway	
Secondary Road	
Railway	++++++++++++
Hiking Trail	- - - - - 🚶
Horse Trail	🐎
Ski Trail	🎿
Campground	⛺
Picnic Area	⛱
Accommodation	🏨
Gasoline	⛽
Information	❓
Warden Station	Ⓦ
Viewpoint	📷
Cabin—closed to public	🏚
Cabin—open to public	🏠

Miles
0   2   4   6   8

km
0 1 2   4   6   8   10

N

● Sorcerer Mtn

● Mystic

Mt C

↑ Eva Lk   N

Heather Lk

P

Ice Box

Mt
Revelstoke

0 50m 100m   200m
0 200ft. 400ft. 600ft.

**MOUNT REVELSTOKE SUMMIT AREA
HIKING TRAILS**

Maunder Ck

Woolsey Ck

Cor

West Woolsey Ck

Hwy
23

St Cyr Ck

● Mt St Cyr

COLUMBIA   **MOUNTAINS**

● Mt Dickey

*CLACHNACUDAINN
ICEFIELD*

● Mt Coursier

● Mt Klotz

CLACHNACUDAINN
RANGE

Coursier Ck

Eva
Lk

Mt
Williamson

Miller Lk

Lower
Jade Lk

Upper
Jade Lk

Clachnacudainn Ck

Skunk Cabbage
picnic area

Mt
Revelstoke

Eagle Lk

Balsam
Lk

Hamilton Ck

**Park
Gate**

Illecillewaet R

Summit
Road

Bridge
Ck

Ⓦ ❓

to Kamloops

City of Revelstoke

MOUNT REVELSTOKE
NATIONAL PARK

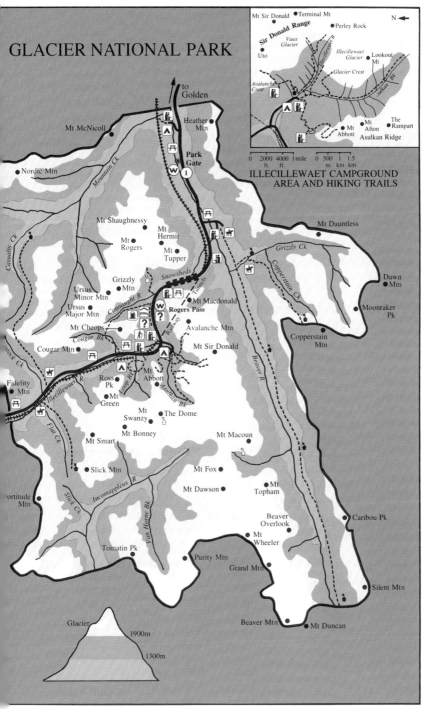

SCENIC DRIVES AND VIEWPOINTS

The Trans-Canada Highway through Mount Revelstoke and Glacier national parks and the Summit Road up Mount Revelstoke offer outstanding opportunities to enjoy scenic drives through the mountains.

All vehicles stopping in the parks require a vehicle permit. These can be purchased throughout the year at the Rogers Pass Information Centre, park offices and gates. During the winter, permits also are issued at the east gate of Glacier.

Scenery at the summit of Rogers Pass attracts tourists from around the world. Numerous viewpoints along both sides of the highway provide opportunities to stop and enjoy the magnificent views. Although the road is open year-round, these viewpoints are usually snow free only from May through October.

During the avalanche control season—usually from November through April—the highway may be closed for avalanche shoots. These closures are usually short (three hours or less), but occasionally they extend for several days. You must carefully obey all warning signs while driving through the parks in winter. Winter snow tires or well-fitting tire chains are required during the winter months.

The Rogers Pass Information Centre at the summit of Rogers Pass is open throughout the year to provide motorists with park information.

The Summit Road up Mount Revelstoke is one of the few roads in Canada where you can drive to the summit of a mountain, but generally this is possible only from July through September. In winter only the first 2 km of the road are plowed. During October and November and again during May and June expect the road to be open part way to the top. From December through April it is closed near the base. There is no public transportation up the Summit Road, but you can hire a taxi in Revelstoke to make the trip.

PICNICKING

Six picnic areas in Glacier and four in Mount Revelstoke are scattered along park roadsides at convenient intervals. Most combine interpretive viewpoints, and some, such as Giant Cedars and Skunk Cabbage have nature trails. Picnic areas are opened as soon as snowmelt permits. In Glacier, this means a season from June through October. In Mount Revelstoke, Giant Cedars and Skunk Cabbage have a season from May through October; Five Mile and Balsam Lake picnic areas along the Summit Road are accessible as soon as the road opens.

BUS TOURS

Numerous tour bus companies operate on the Trans-Canada Highway through the parks. A highlight of this trip is the drive through Rogers Pass and a stop at the Rogers Pass Information Centre. The main tour season is

Rogers Pass Information Centre

from May through October; your travel agent will have details. Regularly scheduled commercial buses stop at the summit of Rogers Pass and in the city of Revelstoke. A special information package called the *Guide's Guide* and *Bus Stop* has been prepared by the parks for bus tour drivers and escorts. Drivers can obtain copies at the Rogers Pass Information Centre or by writing the parks.

BICYCLING
Each year hundreds of cross-country cyclists pass through the area. All cyclists must stay on either the Trans-Canada Highway or Summit Road while in the parks. Cyclists wishing to spend the night in the parks are cautioned that Illecillewaet and Loop Campgrounds are usually full from mid-afternoon during July and August. Mountain Creek Campground, 21 km east of Rogers Pass, usually is not crowded.

The Summit Road from km 1.6 to km 26 is hard surfaced gravel suitable for mountain bike travel, but note that mountain bikes are permitted only on some park trails. Inquire at park offices.

RAILWAY TRAVEL
Via Rail operates a daily passenger service through Glacier National Park, but there are no passenger stations within the park. The closest stations are in Golden and Revelstoke. The observation cars provide a relaxing way to view park scenery. Take careful note of the daylight hours listed in A Columbia Mountains Calendar (pp. 102–121) and make sure that your train passes through the park during daylight hours. Your travel agent will have details.

JAMES W. MULCHINOCK

A well-prepared skier

CAMPGROUNDS AND HOTELS

Environment Canada–Parks operates three campgrounds in Glacier. Ille-cillewaet and Loop Brook campgrounds have fifty-eight and nineteen sites respectively. They are very popular and often fill up in the early afternoon during July and August. Mountain Creek with 306 sites is rarely crowded, and its pull-through sites make it especially attractive to large recreational vehicles. All three campgrounds provide water, wood and washrooms, but there are no hookups or showers. Mountain Creek has a sani-station. All campgrounds are open from mid-June to at least the Labour Day weekend in September. During May, September and October you can camp at the

Beaver River Picnic Area in Glacier park. Camping permits are required in addition to park vehicle permits.

Although there are no campgrounds in Mount Revelstoke park, private and provincial campgrounds situated on both sides of the park in Revelstoke and at Albert Canyon offer a full range of services and are suitable for large and small recreational units. The main camping season is May through October.

For those seeking commercial accommodation, Glacier Park Lodge located beside the Rogers Pass Information Centre is open year-round. The lodge complex includes a year-round service station and towing service, and a small grocery store which is only open during the summer months. Regularly scheduled commercial buses stop at the lodge. Full tourist services are available in the city of Revelstoke and the town of Golden.

WINTER RECREATION
Excellent family-oriented cross-country skiing opportunities exist in Mount Revelstoke. A groomed trail at the base of the Summit Road offers 2-km and 5-km loops with a season extending from December to March. The short loop is illuminated for nighttime skiing. To find the trail, follow the directions to the lower trailhead of the Summit Trail (p. 81). During the same period of the year, the Summit Road is open for skiing from km 1.6 to the Summit at km 26. A picnic shelter at 8 km is stocked with wood and makes an easy lunch stop destination on a day trip. A cabin at km 19.3 and a picnic shelter at Balsam Lake are open for overnight use. You must register at the park office in Revelstoke before any overnight trip. The Summit Trail provides a more direct but steeper route. Snow obscures the trail at higher elevations requiring navigation by map and compass.

Cross-country skiing in Glacier National Park is restricted by steep terrain, avalanche hazard and the avalanche control program. You must register at the Glacier warden office for all skiing in Glacier. Skiing is prohibited on all slopes facing the Trans-Canada Highway during the avalanche control season. Although most skiers use heavy ski mountaineering equipment in Glacier, Asulkan and Balu Pass trails are popular cross-country destinations. Among ski mountaineers, the park is famous for its deep powder routes. Certified mountain guides can be hired in the town of Golden or city of Revelstoke to lead ski trips into the backcountry.

Although skiing is the more popular winter activity in Mount Revelstoke and Glacier, most park trails also are suitable for snowshoeing. In Mount Revelstoke park, Inspiration Woods, Giant Cedars and Skunk Cabbage are good trails for short snowshoe trips. In Glacier, a snowshoe into the Illecillewaet Campground area from the winter parking area provides a few hours of winter recreation. All snowshoers in Glacier park must register at the Glacier warden office.

FISHING AND HUNTING

During the national park open seasons, you can fish for rainbow trout, brook trout, cutthroat trout, Dolly Varden and mountain whitefish in park waters. You must obtain a special national parks fishing licence and a copy of the annual regulations from a park office. Please note that provincial regulations and licences do not apply in national parks. Although productivity is very low in most park waters, some sport fishing can be enjoyed in the alpine lakes in Mount Revelstoke and in the major rivers in Glacier.

No hunting is permitted in these national parks. If you have a gun in your vehicle, it must be securely wrapped or carried in a closed case, or dismantled. You may not carry a gun in the backcountry.

SWIMMING AND BOATING

Park waters generally are too cold to attract water sports enthusiasts. Occasionally, spells of warm weather may make a quick dip in an alpine lake tolerable. Public swimming is available at the City of Revelstoke's municipal pool or in Albert Canyon at Canyon Hotsprings. Canoeing and kayaking on local rivers require whitewater experience and should only be attempted by experts.

ROCK HOUNDING

Although you are not allowed to collect rock samples in the parks, you are welcome to enjoy looking for the various minerals found in these mountains. A detailed road log to geological points of interest along the Trans-Canada Highway through Glacier and Mount Revelstoke is contained in *Field Guides to Geology and Mineral Deposits in the Southern Canadian Cordillera* by Price, et al. See Suggested Reading, p. 124.

HANG GLIDING AND SCENIC FLYING

No hang gliding is permitted in the parks. You can charter aircraft in either Revelstoke or Golden for scenic flights over the parks. There are no airstrips within the parks, and it is not legal to land a helicopter in them. Low-altitude flying is discouraged in order not to disturb wildlife or disrupt the wilderness experience. Contact a park office for details on minimum flight elevations.

SCHOOL TRIPS AND PARK STUDIES

The Park Interpretation section provides assistance to teachers wishing to bring their classes to the parks or to study the parks in the classroom setting. Experienced staff are prepared to take classes on nature hikes or historical tours. A study guide and filmstrip on the parks is available from the Rogers Pass Information Centre.

THE FRIENDS OF MOUNT REVELSTOKE & GLACIER

Members of this nonprofit group help people appreciate, understand and enjoy the heritage of these two parks. They sponsor special events and environmental education projects and sell related publications. Those interested in joining can contact any of the parks' offices.

PHOTOGRAPHY IN MOUNT REVELSTOKE AND GLACIER

The parks offer outstanding opportunities to photograph wilderness mountain scenery. The following tips should help you obtain better photographs.

1. Exposures of snow scenes are difficult. Since the parks are snow-covered much of the time, the problem of snow scene photography is a common one. If you let your camera light meter point at a snow surface, it will give you a reading that will result in too dark an exposure. Increase all readings off snow by one and a half f stops. For example, if your meter reads f16, the best exposure will be about f8/f11. Alternatively, take your light reading from the sky, the asphalt road surface, or use the general guidelines provided by the film manufacturers.
2. Do not use a polarizing filter above 2000 metres or your photographs will likely appear too blue.
3. A moderate telephoto lens (e.g. 80–200 mm) will work best for general photography. If you use a standard or wide angle lens (e.g. 28–55 mm) for scenery, the mountains may look disappointingly small in your photographs.
4. Excellent photographs of the alpine wildflowers can be had by visiting the summit of Mount Revelstoke during the first or second weeks of August. A slightly overcast day will produce more vivid colours in your pictures than a bright sunny day. If you have a tripod and an umbrella, try photographing the flowers during a light rain shower.

PARK INFORMATION

Park Offices

Environment Canada–Parks welcomes detailed questions on park resources, services and facilities. Address your inquiries to:

The Superintendent
Mount Revelstoke and Glacier National Parks
301 Campbell Avenue
Box 350, Revelstoke, B.C.
V0E 2S0
(604/837-5155)

The parks' office is located in downtown Revelstoke. It is open year-round during normal working hours.

Park interpretation staff are specially trained to provide details on the human and natural history of the area. Based in the Rogers Pass Information Centre, they maintain an extensive collection of natural history specimens, artifacts, scientific publications and photographs. Visitors are welcome to use the Centre's library. The building, open all year, is located on the Trans-Canada Highway near the summit of Rogers Pass in Glacier. You can contact the Centre directly by phoning (604) 837-6274.

Visitor services staff also are based in the Rogers Pass Information Centre from early May to late October. They can provide you with a wide range of current information on recreational opportunities in the parks and the region. From them you can buy vehicle permits, topographical maps and national park fishing licences.

The Glacier park warden office is located directly across the highway from the Centre. This is the place to go for information and advice on mountaineering, glacier travel, caving and registration.

Regional Travel Information

The provincial government publishes a comprehensive travel guide to the province on a yearly basis. The guide contains information on all provincial parks, accommodations and services in the Revelstoke-Golden areas. You can obtain a copy by contacting:

Tourism B.C.
1117 Wharf Street
Victoria, B.C.
V8W 2Z2
(604/387-1642)

BRUCE HAGGERSTONE

Conducted hike on Mount Revelstoke

For additional local information on non-park services and recreational opportunities, contact the regional tourist association:

High Country Tourist Association
Box 298
670 – 11th Avenue N.E.
Salmon Arm, B.C.
V0E 2T0
(604/832-8028)

Maps

Special topographic maps are available for both parks. The parks also are covered by the standard topographical series at a scale of 1:50,000. The Hiking Trails section of this book (pp. 81 – 101) lists the appropriate sheets for each hiking route. You can obtain maps at the Rogers Pass Information Centre, the park office in Revelstoke or by writing:

Geological Survey of Canada
6th Floor, 100 West Pender Street
Vancouver, B.C.
V6B 1R8

Aerial Photographs

The most recent complete aerial photography was done in 1978. Partial or complete photography also is available for earlier years. Reference copies of all photographs can be viewed in the Rogers Pass Information Centre. You can order aerial photographs from:

National Air Photo Library
615 Booth Street
Ottawa, Ontario
K1A 0E9
(613/995-4560)

Films

Two films about this area are on view at the Rogers Pass Information Centre. *Snow War* shows the action behind the scenes of the avalanche control operation in Rogers Pass and is available in either video cassette or 16 mm format. It can be borrowed or purchased from the National Film Board of Canada, Box 6100, Montreal, Quebec H3C 3H5. *Underground Rivers* features the Nakimu Caves area of Glacier park and can be purchased from the NFB.

IMPORTANT PARK REGULATIONS
- All natural and historical features in the parks are protected.
- All vehicles stopping in the parks must have a park permit.
- No off-road camping is permitted within 3 km of a road.
- No guns are allowed in the backcountry.
- Provincial fishing licences are not valid in national parks.
- Mountain bikes and motorcycles are not allowed on park trails.
- Visitors must register out and in with the park warden service for all overnight backcountry trips, climbing trips and ski mountaineering trips. (Registrations are not required for day hikes on park trails or day ski trips on the Mount Revelstoke cross-country ski trails.)

HIKING TRAILS

MOUNT REVELSTOKE NATIONAL PARK

Summit Trail

Length:	10 km (one way)
Hiking time:	4 to 5 hours (uphill)
Elevation range:	600 m to 1830 m (+1230 m)
Lower Trailhead:	edge of the lot marked for trailer parking at the base of the Summit Road
Upper Trailhead:	beside the Balsam Lake warden cabin at the junction of the Balsam Lake picnic area road and the Summit Road
Map:	Mount Revelstoke 82 M/1

This old trail, which leads from the base of Mount Revelstoke to the summit, dates from the turn of the century and was the first route to the now famous wildflower meadows of the park.

Summit Trail gives hikers a cross-sectional look at the life zones in the Columbia Mountains. Starting from the interior cedar-hemlock forest, it climbs through the lower subalpine and ends in the upper subalpine. The floral meadows at the summit are usually at their best in early August.

At the lower trailhead you can see the remains of an abandoned ski jump on the left. As you hike the first part of the trail, you pass through the overgrown runs of a former downhill ski development. Recreational skiing dates back to 1892 when local citizens began using the slopes. The ski jump was internationally rated and the scene of several world record-breaking jumps during international competitions. Today, trails at the base of the mountain are still popular with cross-country skiers. Commercial downhill facilities are now located outside the park at Mount Mackenzie.

Starting from the lower trailhead, you will cross the Summit Road in six locations. At the seventh meeting with the road, the trail follows the Summit Road for 1.2 km. Watch for trail signs on the left. After a short final section through the forest, the trail ends beside the Balsam Lake warden cabin. The road continues to the summit of Mount Revelstoke. Some hikers prefer to hike the trail from the top down.

Inspiration Woods Trail

Length:	4 km (round trip)
Hiking time:	1½ hours
Elevation:	610 m (minimal change)
Trailhead:	at the first switchback on the Mount Revelstoke Summit Road
Map:	Mount Revelstoke 82 M/1

This pleasant forest walk suits its poetic name. Trees typical of the interior cedar-hemlock forest such as western hemlock, western white pine and Douglas-fir line the trail. The trail is noted for its display of mushrooms in September and October, but please remember that mushroom collecting is not permitted in national parks. Caribou use this type of cedar-hemlock forest as early winter habitat. Its low elevation makes Inspiration Woods a popular hike both early (April–May) or late (October–November) in the season. The trail has a looped end; you will be able to return to the trailhead by carefully following the directional arrows and ignoring disused sections of old trail and road.

Lindmark Trail

Length:	8 km (one way)
Hiking time:	3½ hours (uphill)
Elevation range:	875 m to 1830 m (+955 m)
Lower Trailhead:	across from the first picnic area along the Mount Revelstoke Summit Road about 8 km from the base
Upper Trailhead:	Balsam Lake Picnic Shelter
Map:	Mount Revelstoke 82 M/1

Revelstoke Mayor C. F. Lindmark was an early booster of the scenic values of Mount Revelstoke. Support by local citizens, including the mayor, led to the establishment of this national park in 1914. Place names such as Miller Lake, Eva Lake, Hamilton Creek and Mount Dickey commemorate this community interest.

Lindmark trail traverses the same life zones as Summit Trail but has the advantage of not crossing the Summit Road. Hikers can follow the trail from either end. Just below the upper trailhead is a small subalpine lake locally known as Eagle Lake. It is only 1.5 m deep and has no fish. By late summer its waters are often warm enough for a refreshing swim.

Balsam Lake, at the upper trailhead, owes its name to the many fir trees along its shoreline. These are actually subalpine fir but were once confused with balsam fir—a distinct species common across much of Canada but not found in southern British Columbia. There are no fish in the lake and its deepest point is only 1 m.

Camping at Eva Lake

JOHN G. WOODS

Eva Lake Trail

Length:	6 km (one way)
Hiking time to the lake:	2 hours
Elevation range:	1920 m to 1936 m (rolling terrain, +16 m)
Trailhead:	at the upper end of the Summit Road
Map:	Mount Revelstoke 82 M/1

This trail, named after Eva Hobbs, an active early member of the Revelstoke Mountaineering Club, crosses gently rolling country in the upper subalpine zone just below the treeless alpine. In some places, the trail passes through strips of stunted subalpine fir, mountain hemlock and Engelmann spruce. Where local conditions inhibit tree growth, the trail skirts and crosses meadows which in August are carpeted with subalpine wildflowers.

About 5.5 km from the trailhead there is a junction with Miller Lake and Jade Lakes trails. The left branch leads to Eva Lake, a good lunch stop. A rustic cabin is open to the public, and overnight camping is permitted. Open fires are not allowed here, so pack a small stove.

Although fish are not native to any of the high-elevation lakes in the parks, the cutthroat and brook trout easily seen in the shallow waters are from stocks placed in the lake in 1933 and 1963 respectively. The stocking program has now been discontinued. Brook trout up to twenty years old have been collected in Eva Lake, but their growth rate is exceptionally poor, and few fish grow larger than 200 g. Their weight actually declines after seven to ten years. Eva Lake has a maximum depth of only 12 m and is usually ice-free from mid-July to mid-October.

An indistinct trail around the water's edge leads to an impressive viewpoint looking north across the Coursier Creek valley.

Miller Lake Trail

Length:	5.5 km (one way)
Hiking time to the lake:	2 hours
Elevation range:	1920 m to 1900 m (rolling terrain, − 20 m)
Trailhead:	same as Eva Lake trail
Map:	Mount Revelstoke 82 M/1

At the turn of the century school inspector A. E. Miller explored the park area and wrote articles in the Revelstoke newspaper extolling the region's scenic beauties. This alpine lake, named in his honour, continues to be a favourite day-hike destination. During the last ice age a glacier sat in the basin now filled by the lake. The moving sheet of ice ate away at the depression and formed this bowl-shaped cirque.

The beginning of this hike follows the same trail as Eva Lake. At a junction about 5.4 km from the start, the trail to the right leads to Miller Lake. A point jutting into the water makes an ideal lunch stop. Overnight camping is not permitted.

This naturally barren lake was first stocked with cutthroat trout in 1933 and brook trout in 1967 but stocking has been discontinued. It has a maximum depth of 27 m, and is usually ice free from mid-July to late October.

Jade Lakes Trail

Length:	9 km (one way)
Hiking time to the lakes:	3½ hours
Elevation range:	1825 m to 2160 m (rolling terrain, +335 m)
Trailhead:	upper end of the Summit Road
Map:	Mount Revelstoke 82 M/1

The jade-green waters of the Upper and Lower Jade Lakes have been photographed countless times by hikers with the strength to climb over the pass leading from Miller Lake to the Jade Lakes.

Follow the route described for the Eva Lake Trail as far as the junction (5.4 km from the trailhead). Take the trail leading straight ahead. This trail ascends the steep ridge above Miller Lake. Near the summit of the pass you enter the treeless alpine tundra with its far-reaching views of mountains and valleys. This is the home of the golden eagle and golden-mantled ground squirrel.

Many hikers call it a day at the summit of the pass and spend some time here enjoying the commanding views of the lakes below. Energetic hikers may continue down the other side of the pass on a steep trail which becomes indistinct near the lakes. Overnight camping is permitted.

Both lakes were first stocked with rainbow trout in 1941, and brook trout were introduced into Upper Jade in 1967. Neither lake is now stocked. Like most of these park waters, the Jade Lakes are very poor in nutrients and have an impoverished invertebrate life. The fish grow very slowly but tend to be exceptionally long-lived. A nineteen-year-old trout from Lower Jade is the oldest rainbow ever recorded in the Canadian mountain parks and may be a world age record for the species. Scientists determined its age by counting annual growth rings on a cross section of the fish's otolith—a tiny ear bone.

Upper Jade Lake has a maximum depth of 14 m and a typical ice-free period from late July to mid-October. Lower Jade reaches a depth of 23 m and is usually open from early July to late October.

Mountain Meadows

Length:	1 km (round trip)
Hiking time:	½ hour
Elevation:	1920 m (minimal change)
Trailhead:	south side of the Heather Lake parking lot at the upper end of the Summit Road
Map:	Mount Revelstoke 82 M/1

This nature trail consists of a short loop through the upper subalpine meadows and forests typical of the Columbia Mountains.

Starting with the yellow avalanche lilies and white spring beauties in late July, the floral show culminates in an August kaleidoscope of red Indian paintbrush, white mountain valerian, yellow arnica, purple lupine and pink mountain daisies. Between the meadows the trail crosses stands of stunted subalpine fir. Benches are provided at two viewpoints. The trail features a close look at the Icebox—a crevice in the rock perpetually filled with snow, which was featured in Ripley's "Believe It Or Not" column in 1933.

Mountain Meadows and other pathways in the summit area have been hard-surfaced to encourage hikers to stay on trails thus protecting the delicate high elevation vegetation. In an ecological study of human impact on high elevation meadows in the 1970s, scientists identified a severe overuse problem. Following their recommendations, in 1975 the meadows were rehabilitated by reconstructing the trails and transplanting native vegetation onto the damaged sites. With public co-operation, this experiment in alpine revegetation has worked well, and the meadows continue to be renowned for their scenic beauty.

Skunk cabbage leaves in summer

Skunk Cabbage Trail

Length: 1.2 km (round trip)
Hiking time: ½ hour
Elevation: 610 m (minimal change)
Trailhead: Skunk Cabbage Picnic Area, Trans-Canada High-
                       way. The trail starts within the picnic area near the
                       river
Map: Illecillewaet 82 N/4

This nature trail allows you to explore the swamplands along the Illecil-lewaet River (an Indian word meaning "rushing river" and pronounced "Illy-silly-what"). It features a boardwalk with observation platforms and signs explaining the diverse vegetation and wildlife of the area.

From late April to mid-May the yellow spikes of flowering skunk cabbage brighten the trailside. The swamp is an excellent area for birdwatching especially during May and June when rufous hummingbirds are conspicuously abundant. Black-headed grosbeaks, rare elsewhere in the parks, are regularly seen here, and song sparrows and common yellowthroats provide a constant background of bird song. Look for American dippers along the small creek at the start of the trail. Beaver and muskrat are very active in the swamp and can often be observed.

In 1983 and again in 1984 the small creek at the start of the trail became a raging torrent, flooding the highway above the trail and diverging through the swamps. Although a dramatic event at the time, the geographic record shows us that such unpredictable stream flow and low elevation flooding are frequent events in the history of these mountains.

Giant Cedars Trail

Length:	0.5 km (round trip)
Hiking time:	15 minutes
Elevation:	700 m (minimal change)
Trailhead:	across from the picnic shelter in Giant Cedars picnic area on the north side of the Trans-Canada Highway near the eastern boundary of Mount Revelstoke National Park
Map:	Illecillewaet 82 N/4

Few people realize that there is a rainforest of giant trees far from the coast of British Columbia. Along this short boardwalk you will see huge western red cedar trees typical of mature cedar-hemlock forests in the Columbia Mountains. Signs along the walk identify major plant species.

The rivulet running through the forest is an important drinking place for at least four species of bats. In the evening, just as night falls, there is a flurry of activity as the bats fly down for a drink. If you sit very quietly on the boardwalk beside this trickle of water, you may see these creatures flitting over quiet pools in the woodland. During the day, the bats probably roost high in the cedars.

Steller's jays are usually conspicuous at Giant Cedars from April through November. These long-lived, blue-and-black birds haunt the same area of woods year after year. Some have frequented this picnic area for six years or more.

GLACIER NATIONAL PARK

Bostock Creek Trail

Length:	9 km (one way)
Hiking time:	3½ hours (uphill)
Elevation range:	1021 m to 1753 m (+732 m)
Trailhead:	on the north side of the Trans-Canada Highway, 4 km east of the western park boundary
Map:	Illecillewaet 82 N/4, Glacier 82 N/5

Caribou once passed through this valley in large numbers and the original name, Caribou Creek, was appropriate. Caribou are no longer abundant anywhere in the park although a few are seen each winter north of Bostock Pass. The valley name was changed in 1896 to honour a Canadian senator.

Bostock Creek trail offers a moderate hike through the interior cedar-hemlock forest, across the lower subalpine and into the upper subalpine. At first, views are restricted to Mount Fidelity and Corbin Peak. Careful observers will spot the odd-shaped white hut of the Christiania snow research station on the ridge running east from Mount Fidelity.

Christiania Snow Research Field Station

At the summit of the pass hikers have the opportunity to see one of the few areas in the park where sedimentary rock covers the older and harder metamorphic bedrock typical of the Columbia Mountains. This blanket of limestone and shales gives the summit a distinctively different look and feel. The pass is an excellent destination for an overnight backpacking trip. From here you can explore relatively gentle alpine tundra ridges.

Cougar Valley Trail

Length:	4.8 km (one way)
Hiking time:	2 hours (uphill)
Elevation range:	1098 m to 1878 m (+780 m)
Trailhead:	on the northeast edge of the bridge over Cougar Brook on the Trans-Canada Highway, 9 km west of the Rogers Pass Centre
Map:	Glacier 82 N/5

Cougar Brook is a name of local origin referring to the mountain lions that were once said to frequent this valley, though it is unlikely that these large cats ever were abundant here. One of the few park sightings of cougar in recent years occurred in this valley in 1965.

A principal attraction of Cougar Valley trail is the Nakimu Caves, one of the largest underground cave systems in Canada with some 5.8 km of passageways. Although the caves themselves are closed to the public, old trails above them lead to a variety of interesting surface features such as disappearing and reappearing streams, collapsed gorges and sink holes. For more information on the caves you can view an exhibit in the Rogers Pass

Scalloped bedrock in Nakimu Caves

Information Centre and see *Underground Rivers,* a movie about caves.

From the trailhead, follow a steep switchbacking trail for about 500 m through the heavy rainforest until you reach a relatively open old roadbed. Turn uphill and follow the road out of the forest and across huge avalanche paths. Be wary: this is grizzly country.

At the trail end, the old path to the caves leads straight ahead. To the right, a steep trail connects with Balu Pass trail. From this point Balu Pass summit is a 3.9-km hike with an elevation gain of 222 m.

The connection between the Cougar and Balu Pass trails allows you to hike them as a single long hike. Many hikers start on the Balu Pass Trail then return to the highway via the Cougar Valley Trail. To do this, you will need to park a car at the Cougar Valley trailhead since the trailheads are several kilometres apart.

Loop Trail

Length:	1.6 km (round trip)
Hiking time:	1 hour
Elevation:	1190 m (minimal change)
Trailhead:	at the highway viewpoint just east of Loop Brook campground
Map:	Glacier 82 N/5

Named after the famous loops of the original railway grade over Rogers Pass, Loop trail offers an easy one-hour circle tour with numerous viewpoints and features of interest. Signs with texts and historic photographs will help you relive the story of the first Canadian Pacific Railway line across these mountains. The trail also provides an exceptional view of the glacier-studded north face of Mount Bonney.

After a short series of switchbacks through the forest, the trail follows the abandoned railway line generally downhill. A large loop will bring you back to your car. Follow the directional arrows very closely; avoid side trails and roads into the campground.

Avalanche Crest Trail

Length: 4.2 km (one way)
Hiking time: 3 hours (uphill)
Elevation range: 1250 m to 2045 m (+795 m)
Trailhead: behind Illecillewaet campground. Follow the hiker signs to the cabin behind the campground. Across the road a major trailhead sign indicates the start of the trail.
Map: Blaeberry 82 N/6

From November through May each year this crest spawns numerous avalanches which threaten the Trans-Canada Highway. The treeless slopes stretching down the mountain offer proof to summer hikers of this winter phenomenon.

Experienced hikers rate Avalanche Crest among the best scenic trails in the park. Unparalleled views of Rogers Pass, Hermit Range, Illecillewaet River valley, Mount Bonney, Asulkan Brook valley and the perpetual ice of the Illecillewaet Névé compensate for the strenuous uphill climb.

Hikers can see the original route of the Canadian Pacific Railway as it loops up towards the headwater area of the Illecillewaet River. It is from somewhere in the vicinity of Avalanche Crest that Major Rogers first viewed this famous pass in 1881.

Soon after leaving the road, Avalanche Crest trail branches off to the left. Ancient western red cedar and huge Engelmann spruce line its first section. The trail continues uphill; at about 1.6 km you can take a short spur to the left leading to a viewpoint.

As you continue up the main trail, the country becomes more open in the upper subalpine zone. Be careful not to take one of the old trails leading off to the right. If you look at the mountains above you when you reach the first creek crossing, you may be able to see a bulge on the ridge to the right in the shape of an eagle. The mountain is appropriately named Eagle Peak.

The trail emerges into an open alpine basin nestled between Avalanche Crest to the left and a ridge from Eagle Peak to the right. If conditions are favourable, many hikers pick their own route up the crest (2375 m) and enjoy a panoramic view from the high country. Typical summer birds here include golden eagles, water pipits and rosy finches. Hoary marmots are often seen in the rock piles.

Climber hiking towards peaks in the Sir Donald Range

Sir Donald Trail

Length:	4 km (one way)
Hiking time:	2½ hours (uphill)
Elevation range:	1250 m to 2165 m (+915 m)
Trailhead:	behind Illecillewaet Campground (see Avalanche Crest Trail)
Map:	Blaeberry 82 N/6

Mount Sir Donald is named for Sir Donald A. Smith, the famous Canadian Pacific Railway director who drove the last spike on the CPR at Craigellachie in 1885. Typical of most trails in the Illecillewaet River valley, this one was originally built by the railway as an access route for mountain climbers. Mount Sir Donald is a classic climb, and the trail leading to its base is a rigorous uphill hike. If you are looking for a way to test your wind and energy, this trail is for you.

Follow signs indicating the Sir Donald and Perley Rock trails. After a gentle start, the route steepens. Past a series of switchbacks, it crosses an avalanche path strewn with trees knocked down by a snowslide in 1972.

Look for pikas where trails pass through boulder piles

Minor creeks are crossed in several locations; then the turbulent creek formed by the meltwaters of the Vaux Glacier is crossed at 2.2 km. At 0.3 km past this crossing, the trail reaches a junction. The Sir Donald Trail continues ahead and the Perley Rock Trail branches right. From this point to the trail end, in the basin before Vaux Glacier, the hiking is extremely rugged, with the 3297-m horn of Mount Sir Donald looming above you.

Vaux Glacier has been advancing in recent years, and its snout is very steep. Stay well back from the ice—rock and ice falls are a real danger here. On the face of Sir Donald, lighter-coloured rock shows where a major rockslide released during the summer of 1983. Hikers will note a faint trail on the lateral moraine to the left. This is the route used by climbers challenging Mount Sir Donald's famous northwest ridge.

Perley Rock Trail

Length:	5.6 km (one way)
Hiking time:	3 hours (uphill)
Elevation range:	1250 m to 2147 m (+897 m); elevation at Perley Rock summit 2412 m
Trailhead:	behind Illecillewaet Campground (see Avalanche Crest Trail)
Map:	Blaeberry 82 N/6

H. A. Perley undoubtedly sent Glacier House guests up to this area of the park many times during his tenure as hotel manager in the early days of the park. The Canadian Pacific Railway removed the hotel in 1929, but hikers can see its foundations and enjoy the trip to Perley Rock.

This is an ambitious hike. Follow the route as described for the Sir Donald Trail, but at the junction take the right branch. The trail ends before the summit of Perley Rock. From the trail end, hike uphill and locate an old portion of the trail switchbacking madly uphill. Perley Rock is the low knoll visible ahead. Head for the lowest point on the left side of the knoll and carefully make your way across the steep snow slopes and boulders. Snow crossings are exceedingly dangerous—one slip and you could slide into the rock pile below and be seriously injured.

The summit of Perley Rock offers an unsurpassed view of the expanse of the Illecillewaet Névé. Look for white-tailed ptarmigan and rosy finches around the margins of the rock. *Under no conditions* should you walk onto the ice without proper mountaineering gear; and do not forget that registration with the park warden service is required before any glacier travel.

Great Glacier Trail

Length:	4.8 km (one way)
Hiking time:	2 to 3 hours (uphill)
Elevation range:	1250 m to 1570 m (+320 m); elevation at glacier snout: 1935 m
Trailhead:	behind Illecillewaet campground. Follow hiker signs to the cabin behind the campground. Turn right at the cabin and follow the road across the Illecillewaet River. The trailhead will be obvious a short way ahead on the left beside the Glacier House sign.
Map:	Blaeberry 82 N/6, Mount Wheeler 82 N/3

The "Great Glacier," now called the Illecillewaet, has been a well-known landmark to visitors in this region since the 1880s. At that time a giant tongue of ice protruded deeply into the valley, and a hike to the icy snout was a short stroll from the railway. Today, things have changed. Over the past century the ice front has receded about 1.5 km upslope. However, during the last decade the glacier's snout has been enlarging and pushing down the valley at a rate of about 10 m per year. Despite this new advance, the ice is still a long way above the trailhead.

After following a gentle grade through the forest, you will cross a major avalanche path. The larger boulders in this opening are a favoured haunt of the American pika, a small, rabbit-like mammal. Past the slide path you will ascend a fairly steep lateral moraine. This gravel ridge once flanked the glacier. Near the trail end, the scoured and scraped bedrock is a reminder that glacial ice very recently occupied this area. Walk cautiously: when wet this bedrock can be very slippery.

The trail ends at the exposed bedrock well below the glacier. An hour of rigorous rock scrambling will bring you to the glacier's snout. Sturdy hiking boots are advisable. Be prepared for sudden changes in the weather. At the ice front, stay clear of the areas of falling ice. Proper glacier-crossing gear and registration with the park warden service are required for parties proceeding onto the ice.

Glacier Crest Trail

Length:	4.8 km (one way)
Hiking time:	3 hours (uphill)
Elevation range:	1250 m to 2045 m (+795 m); elevation of crest: 2255 m
Trailhead:	behind Illecillewaet Campground (see Great Glacier Trail)
Maps:	Blaeberry 82 N/6, Mount Wheeler 82 N/3

As the name suggests, Glacier Crest offers glacier views on both of its flanks—the giant tongue of the Illecillewaet to the east and the irregular walls of the Asulkan Glacier to the west. The ridge itself is an arête carved by the glaciers that once flowed down the valleys on either side.

From the trailhead, follow the directional signs. After a gentle climb through dense forest, the trail crosses Asulkan Brook. Just past this crossing, the Glacier Crest Trail veers to the left and begins a steady switchbacking ascent. The trail end offers a good view of the Asulkan Brook valley. When conditions are favourable, many hikers carefully pick their own routes to the summit of the crest. The view from this alpine spine is a Columbia Mountain panorama of rock and glacial ice.

Asulkan Valley Trail

Length:	6.5 km (one way)
Hiking time:	4 hours (uphill)
Elevation range:	1250 m to 2175 m (+925 m)
Trailhead:	behind Illecillewaet Campground (see Great Glacier Trail)
Maps:	Blaeberry 82 N/6, Mount Wheeler 82 N/3

Writing of this valley in 1905, cartographer and explorer Arthur O. Wheeler described the Asulkan as "a gem of mountain scenery. The valley feels enchanted. There is magic in the atmosphere." Glacier views, mountain scenery, waterfalls and a pleasant valley walk through forests and

June in the upper Asulkan valley

across avalanche paths combine to make the Asulkan an excellent introduction to this part of the Columbia Mountains.

The Asulkan valley trail starts beside the Glacier House sign behind Illecillewaet campground. The gently rising trail passes a number of junctions with other trails. Follow the trail signs carefully.

This part of the route is in the transition zone between the interior cedar-hemlock forest and the lower subalpine. Trees typical of both zones line the trail. If you look carefully, you will see western and mountain hemlock growing side by side.

At 1.2 km a footbridge crosses Asulkan Brook. The name Asulkan was first used by William Spotswood Green, an early mountaineer. It reportedly means "wild goat" in one of the Indian dialects and recognizes the abundance of mountain goats he saw at the end of this valley in Asulkan Pass.

After crossing the brook, the trail continues up the Asulkan valley and across several avalanche paths. Hoary marmots can often be seen sunning themselves beside the trail in this area. The mountain walls across the brook form an impressive backdrop accentuated by a number of waterfalls. The mountain names are fitting: The Ramparts, The Dome, Mount Jupiter. Here and there the glaciers at the end of the valley come into view.

About 4 km from the start of the trail, the gentle terrain is left behind as the trail starts a steep climb towards Asulkan Pass. A large glacier-moulded moraine comes into view, and soon the crevasse-riddled ice front of the Asulkan Glacier commands the far skyline. The trail climbs to a footbridge over the upper reaches of Asulkan Brook, skirts a small stand of subalpine forest, and begins a very steep ascent up the spine of another moraine. By the time you reach the trail end, the lowest ice of the Asulkan Glacier is below you. Note that the side of the moraine facing the glacier is nearly barren—evidence of recent glacial activity—whereas the side away from the glacier is well vegetated.

The trail end makes an excellent lunch stop and a place to view the mountains and glaciers of this area. Hikers will note the bare rock in front of the ice. This marks the area covered by the glacier at the end of the last century. Although the glacier is smaller now, if the Asulkan is following the general trend of park glaciers, it is currently enlarging again.

Meeting of the Waters Trail

Length: 1 km (round trip)
Hiking time: ½ hour (round trip)
Elevation: 1250 m (minimal change)
Trailhead: behind Illecillewaet Campground (see Great Glacier Trail)
Map: Blaeberry 82 N/6

This short stroll leads you on a gentle loop with very little elevation change. The highlight of the route is the confluence of the Illecillewaet River and Asulkan Brook, streams formed by meltwaters from the Illecillewaet and Asulkan glaciers. In summer they carry a milky suspension of glacier silt. The streams are at their raging peak in the late afternoon of a hot August day when increased glacial melting occurs. If you stand in the middle of the bridge you can feel the reverberations as large boulders carried by the floodwater bounce along the stream bed. American dippers can be seen throughout the year bobbing and diving as they hunt invertebrate life in these turbulent flows. Benches are provided at the confluence.

From the trailhead, you follow the Meeting of the Waters loop by taking the left-hand branch at all major trail junctions. Ignore all disused looking pathways. As you follow the Illecillewaet River back toward the campground, watch for a short spur trail on the left leading to an old stone bridge. You will walk over this remnant of the original Canadian Pacific Railway as you return to the trailhead. The river was first crossed by a wooden bridge. In 1898, this impressive stone arch provided a fireproof crossing.

Marion Lake Trail

Length: 2.2 km (one way)
Hiking time: 1½ hours (uphill)
Elevation range: 1250 m to 1675 m (+425 m)
Trailhead: behind Illecillewaet Campground (see Great Glacier Trail)
Map: Blaeberry 82 N/6, Glacier 82 N/5

William Spotswood Green and his companion Rev. Henry Swanzy made Glacier National Park famous as a mountain climbing area in the late nineteenth century. They made their base at Glacier House, and Green named this lake after his daughter, Marion.

There are few lakes in Glacier National Park. Marion Lake sits in a basin gouged out by glaciers during the last ice age. It has a mean depth of 2.2 m, a maximum depth of 5 m and is typically ice-free from early July to mid-October.

In describing his attempt at fishing at the lake, Green wrote: "I incline to the belief that the reason why the fish did not rise was because there were none there." Green was correct. The harsh climate, nutrient-poor waters and inaccessible location have made colonization by fish life impossible. Park personnel tried unsuccessfully to stock the lake with both brook trout and cutthroat trout in the 1940s.

From the trailhead, hike up the main trail to the first junction and take the right-hand trail. Here you leave the valley as the trail relentlessly switchbacks its way up to the lake. At Marion, a short side trail to the right leads to an observation point featuring the Illecillewaet River valley below you to the west and Rogers Pass to the northeast. Cutthroat trout and Dolly Varden are native to the Illecillewaet River.

The rockslide at the far end of the lake is a popular luncheon spot for hikers. The left-hand junction leads up the Abbott Ridge trail.

Abbott Ridge Trail

Length:	5 km (one way)
Hiking time:	4 hours (uphill)
Elevation range:	1250 m to 2290 m (+1040 m)
Trailhead:	an extension of Great Glacier Trail
Maps:	Blaeberry 82 N/6, Glacier 82 N/5, Illecillewaet 82 N/4

Henry Abbott was one of the bold breed of railway men who dared challenge these mountains nearly a century ago. From the top of "Abbott's" ridge you have a panoramic view of the Selkirks and get a bird's eye view of the railway line he helped to build. The glacier-carved horns of the Sir Donald Range command the eastern horizon.

The trail takes you into true alpine tundra—the land above the trees—and ends on a narrow ridge. For strong hikers there are few routes that more closely simulate a mountain-top experience from the security of an established trail.

Icefields of the Illecillewaet Névé stretch to the south while to the west a tumbling glacier clings to the steep face of Mount Bonney. Looking north, the Hermit Range guards the far side of Rogers Pass. From this vantage you get a true picture of Glacier National Park—where half the land is above 1800 m and more than one-tenth is permanently bound in ice and snow.

The Abbott Ridge Trail follows the Marion Lake Trail to the junction at the lake. Take the left fork and follow the trail uphill above the lake. You will come to another junction with a shortcut marked to the right. Hikers without ice axes are advised to use this shortcut, which avoids persistent and dangerous snowpatches often found on the main route. Continue upwards towards the cliff base.

You will pass the Abbott Observatory along the way. This station monitors snow pack and weather conditions and provides data used to analyze avalanche conditions during the winter. The white boxes contain weather-monitoring equipment, and the aluminum screen on the tower shields a precipitation gauge from fierce mountain winds. Snow research and avalanche warning personnel visit the station at least once a week all winter using mountaineering skis fitted with climbing skins which enable them to ski uphill.

The trail continues up through alpine meadows to the base of a cliff, then ascends to the right (north) and follows a good route to the top. Water pipits and rosy finches are often seen near the end of this trail.

Abandoned Rails Trail

Length:	1.2 km (one way)
Hiking time:	½ hour (one way)
Elevation:	1330 m (minimal change)
Trailheads:	at the Summit Monument in Rogers Pass and at the Rogers Pass Centre
Map:	Glacier 82 N/5

This self-guiding historic route along the old railway bed is nearly level and straight—a rare hiking experience in Glacier National Park. The trail is generally suitable for a street-shoe amble and leads to the ruins of a number of abandoned snowsheds. Trail signs explaining the features of interest are illustrated with historic photographs of the Columbias. The trail can be hiked from either end.

Balu Pass Trail

Length:	5 km (one way)
Hiking time:	2 hours (uphill)
Elevation range:	1312 m to 2100 m (+788 m)
Trailhead:	Rogers Pass Centre
Map:	Glacier 82 N/5

You will not likely forget that you are in bear country on this hike. The trail name is derived from the Indian word ''baloo'' meaning bear. The moun-

Near trail's end, Hermit Trail

tains flanking one wall of the valley are called Grizzly Mountain, Ursus (Latin for bear) Major and Ursus Minor. The trail itself traverses wall-to-wall avalanche slopes and ends in alpine meadows—all excellent bear habitat. Stay alert!

The trail starts as a forest walk through a stand of mountain hemlock and an occasional huge Engelmann spruce. Connaught Creek flows gently by the side of the trail and is an excellent place to see American dippers—adventurous birds that hunt for aquatic invertebrates in mountain streams.

After about a half hour you leave the timber behind. The trail constantly crosses the lower portions of avalanche paths up to the end of the valley. The only steep part of the walk is at the end—a short uphill hike to Balu Pass summit. Wildflowers in August and the view of glaciers, icefields and mountain peaks repay the effort.

From the trail end, it is possible to follow another path 3.9 km down the other side of Balu Pass and link up with the Cougar Valley Trail.

Hermit Trail

Length:	2.8 km (one way)
Hiking time:	2 hours (uphill)
Elevation range:	1287 m to 2057 m (+770 m)
Trailhead:	1.5 km north of the Rogers Pass Centre on the west side of the road
Map:	Glacier 82 N/5

For many years Hermit trail has been an access route for climbers into the Hermit Range. From the trail end, climbers proceed to tackle peaks such as

Backpacking above Copperstain Trail

Mount Tupper, Hermit Mountain and Mount Rogers. With an average steepness of 28 per cent, it is a trail to test the strength of the most avid mountain hiker.

This is an excellent trail from which to compare the Selkirk and Purcell ranges of the Columbia Mountains. The massive, angular quartzite peaks of the Selkirks surround you, while the rounded, more subdued landscape of the Purcells is visible through the eastern end of Rogers Pass.

This steep hike begins on the edge of an avalanche path but soon enters the dense subalpine forest. The first good views are at about 1900 m where the trail comes out of the forest. By staying on the main uphill trail, you will reach the indistinct end of the trail in the alpine meadows.

Beaver River Trail

Length:	37 km (one way)
Hiking time:	3 days (one way)
Elevation range:	923 m to 1372 m (+449 m)
Trailhead:	construction of a new railway line through the park has necessitated rerouting the trailhead. Inquire at the Rogers Pass Information Centre for exact details on locating the start of this trail
Maps:	Blaeberry 82 N/6, Mount Wheeler 82 N/3

The Beaver River valley is big tree country. A day hike along the first part of this trail will reveal ancient Engelmann spruce and western red cedar that began life about 1000 years ago. Numerous species of pyrola (wintergreen) grow along the path, adding colour to the forest floor. The Beaver River trail was constructed as a warden patrol route in pre-highway days. Although it does not offer the best views of park mountains, it can be used to get into the park's interior.

Hikers wishing to explore farther should follow the trail up out of the river bottom and onto higher ground. It continues at this higher level to Grizzly Creek but is not maintained to hiking standards past here. Near the creek, the main trail forks right and crosses the stream, continuing to near the southern boundary of the park. Interested backpackers should consult a park warden for details on current conditions.

Copperstain Trail

Length:	16 km (one way)
Hiking time:	6 hours (uphill)
Elevation range:	923 m to 2053 m (+1130 m); Bald Mountain summit 2317 m
Trailhead:	see Beaver River Trail
Map:	Blaeberry 82 N/6

This trail offers access to one of the best backpacking areas in Glacier National Park—the seemingly endless alpine meadows of Bald Mountain. Copperstain Creek drains an area different from the rest of the park. The Purcell Ranges of the Columbia Mountains are relatively subdued mountains underlain by soft shales and schist. They contrast with the glacier-studded resilient crags of the Selkirk Ranges visible across the valley. Alpine breeders such as water pipits, horned larks and rosy finches are often seen here.

Follow the Beaver River Trail to the Grizzly Creek area. Keep left and proceed up the north side of Grizzly Creek and cross the stream at a bridge beside the Grizzly warden cabin. The trail soon swings up the Copperstain Creek valley. Higher up, hikers will notice the Copperstain warden cabin. (Warden cabins are not open to the public.) Hikers will see the charred areas of the "Copperstain Burn" in this area. The numerous deer and elk tracks along the trail are evidence of the rich habitat created by forest fires. The flowers are thick among the silvery snags, and the combination of fire-weed, paintbrush, various asters and in wetter areas, saxifrages, is in marked contrast to the sparse undergrowth beneath the old-growth forest.

From here the trail ascends into the alpine meadows of Bald Mountain. This is wild backpacking country at its best. Although the trail ends, hikers may explore the meadows for their own routes and camping spots.

A COLUMBIA MOUNTAINS CALENDAR

As the seasons cycle, Mount Revelstoke and Glacier national parks present ever-changing opportunities to enjoy the out-of-doors. Here, the complex interplay of mountains and climate create conditions that bring a flush of spring flowers from late March in the valley bottoms to August on the highest alpine meadows. Here it is possible to ski on a sub-zero snowpack in the morning and take a sunbath in the afternoon. Here too, it can rain in January and snow in July.

In general, the parks' climate can be described as cool and wet. Pacific storms, laden with moisture and energy, sweep across the mountains and are forced to rise. As the air ascends, it expands and cools. Air has a reduced ability to carry moisture at low temperatures, so much of the moisture falls in the form of snow and rain. With increasing elevation, the mountains experience increasingly cold weather and heavier precipitation. This difference between valley bottom and summit is so pronounced that you can move from rain forest to glacier in a single day.

The following calendar provides a month-by-month summary of the weather, the activities of nature, and tips on planning the best ways to enjoy your visit to the parks. Because of the variability of weather from year to year, the only way to be sure of conditions is to phone the parks a few days before you plan to arrive. Since the weather changes considerably with elevation, monthly averages are listed for three elevation sites in the parks: low elevation (Revelstoke, 560 m), mid-elevation (Rogers Pass, 1300 m) and high elevation (Mt. Fidelity, 1830 m). Sunrise and sunset times are provided to help you avoid being benighted on a mountain slope or missing the best times for wildlife viewing.

Autumn in the Clachnacudainn valley   ROGERS PASS ARCHIVES

JANUARY

Weather

This is the snowiest month of the year in Rogers Pass. A thick blanket covers the parks from valley bottom to mountain top and replenishes the glaciers. Many glacial crevasses are bridged by snow, and it takes a sharp eye to distinguish the glaciers from the snowpack. January snowstorms produce many avalanches. Although daily temperatures are typically below freezing at all elevations, mild air from a Pacific storm can produce rain showers. Valley cloud frequently obscures the sun at low elevations. Mountaineers with the stamina to ski into the alpine will often climb above the clouds.

January Averages	Revelstoke	Rogers Pass	Mt. Fidelity
Daily High (C)	− 3.8	− 8.7	− 8.0
Daily Low (C)	− 9.8	−14.1	−13.2
Rainfall (mm)	18.9	8.2	2.1
Snowfall (cm)	145.2	227.9	261.1
Days with Rain or Snow	16	21	22
Max. snow on ground (cm)	74	160	260
Mid-month sunrise (PST)		7.49	
Mid-month sunset (PST)		16.09	

Wildlife and Plants

This is a difficult month to observe park animals. Few birds winter in the mountains, though some years large numbers of pine siskins and red crossbills invade the area to eat the seeds of white birch and several coniferous trees. Black-capped chickadees, red-breasted nuthatches and golden-crowned kinglets are among the deep winter standbys, but it is possible to spend entire days in the field without seeing or hearing a single bird. Ravens give us hope of spring as they start their courtship aerial displays in January.

Most plants are dormant and deeply buried in winter, but January is a good month to study the pendulous tree lichens brought within reach by the deep snowpack.

Recreation

Cross-country and ski mountaineering conditions are often excellent this month. Pick a moonlit night for a ski up the Mount Revelstoke Summit Road to the Five Mile Picnic Shelter. From here you can look out across the Columbia River valley and the lights of Revelstoke. Other favourite daytime ski areas are noted on p. 75.

You can obtain information at park offices or at the Rogers Pass Infor-

Pine siskins along the Trans-Canada Highway

JOHN G. WOODS

mation Centre. Snowfall, avalanches and cold can make exploring the parks a challenge this month. Observe all warning signs and make sure you register in and out with the park wardens for all skiing in Glacier park.

FEBRUARY

Weather
Although the parks appear firmly in winter's grip, the lengthening days give promise of spring. Snowfall continues to fuel both the accumulation of the glaciers and avalanches. In places where water trickles over cliffs, huge blue icicles decorate the winter scenery.

February Averages	Revelstoke	Rogers Pass	Mt. Fidelity
Daily High (C)	1.1	− 3.3	− 4.1
Daily Low (C)	− 5.9	− 9.6	− 9.4
Rainfall (mm)	49.7	2.4	0.3
Snowfall (cm)	76.7	177.3	221.8
Days with Rain or Snow	14	18	19
Max. snow on ground (cm)	74	180	300
Mid-month sunrise (PST)		7.04	
Mid-month sunset (PST)		17.05	

February snowpack on Mount Revelstoke

JAMES W. MULCHINOCK

Wildlife and Plants
Except during the years of winter finch invasions, bird watching in February is in the doldrums. Ravens patrol the highways in pairs and can frequently be seen carrying nesting material.

In the sanctuary of their maternal dens, newborn black and grizzly bears suckle. At treeline, bands of caribou have heavily grazed the tree lichens which sustain them during this difficult period. Wolverine, the great wanderers of the Columbia Mountains, travel from valley to valley leaving their broad tracks through the forests, over the high passes and across the avalanche paths.

February storms frequently lash the trees in the upper subalpine with a combination of wind and snow, causing them to assume a variety of highly unusual shapes.

Recreation
This is often the best month for winter photography in both parks and is mid-season for ski mountaineering and cross-country skiing. Try skiing to the top of the Mount Revelstoke Summit Road for a look at the snow-shrouded trees.

Information is available either at park offices or the Rogers Pass Information Centre. Registration is required for all skiing in Glacier and all overnight skiing in Mount Revelstoke.

MARCH

Weather
With the arrival of the equinox and the official start of spring, cold and ice begin to relinquish their grip on the landscape. Daytime highs are often above freezing in the valleys, and occasionally melting temperatures extend to the tops of the mountains. Although snowfall still dominates the highest slopes, there is a good chance that precipitation will be in the form of rain. With the warming weather, avalanches may rupture to the base of the snowpack and leave their muddy remains beside the highway. On clear days, park glaciers reflect the sun in a brilliant display of whiteness.

March Averages	Revelstoke	Rogers Pass	Mt. Fidelity
Daily High (C)	5	1.2	− 2.4
Daily Low (C)	− 3.8	− 7.3	− 8.2
Rainfall (mm)	55.1	11	2.1
Snowfall (cm)	31.4	125.3	195.5
Days with Rain or Snow	15	19	21
Max. snow on ground (cm)	68	190	325
Mid-month sunrise (PST)		6.05	
Mid-month sunset (PST)		17.54	

Wildlife and Plants

Now the pairs of ravens disappear from the roadsides as they commence their annual nesting cycle. In the Columbia forest occasional pairs of great horned owls tend their eggs, while in the subalpine gray jays are preparing to lay. The first migrants from the south, the common crows and varied thrushes, reappear at low elevations.

Most bears are still in their dens, though by the end of the month a few have emerged from hibernation. Caribou, now thin and conspicuously ribbed, are spending their last difficult month of the year in the upper subalpine. The avalanche paths are frequently crossed by the tracks of coyotes searching for an early spring meal: an unwary ptarmigan or the carcass of a mountain goat.

Spring is signalled in the low country by the blooms of beaked hazel and the bold yellow spikes of skunk cabbage emerging from open woodland pools. The hillsides turn purple as the budding white birch prepare to unfurl their leaves.

Recreation

Conditions are often ideal for spring skiing this month. Contact the Rogers Pass Information Centre, the Glacier warden office or the Revelstoke office for information.

APRIL

Weather

Although above-freezing temperatures are experienced at all elevations this month, above 1300 m the weather is still dominated by snow and cold. Spring rain, sunny afternoons and warm air temperatures often trigger avalanches. The entire snowpack may give way to produce a relatively slow flowing, but powerful, spring snowslide. Crevasses in the many park glaciers are often completely bridged by snow making glacier skiing a favourite April recreation.

April Averages	Revelstoke	Rogers Pass	Mt. Fidelity
Daily High (C)	11.8	6.2	2.3
Daily Low (C)	− 0.1	− 3.6	− 4.7
Rainfall (mm)	51.1	27.7	10.1
Snowfall (cm)	17.7	48	114.1
Days with Rain or Snow	10	15	16
Max. snow on ground (cm)	26	185	325
Mid-month sunrise (PST)		4.54	
Mid-month sunset (PST)		18.46	

Wildlife and Plants

While the ravens complete the incubation of their eggs, a myriad of migrant birds pass through the mountains. At the start of the month, conspicuous lines of Canada geese pour up the Columbia river valley along the edge of Mount Revelstoke. Waves of dark-eyed juncos and American robins flood the valleys, moving higher up into the mountains as the month advances. Each April, Steller's jays line the Trans-Canada Highway in a cycle of showiness that may represent a form of migration. On warm afternoons, butterflies, such as the mourning cloak and Milbert's tortoise shell, emerge from their hiding places, find a convenient twig or leaf, and bask in the sun. On any mild day, troops of snow scorpionflies march across the deteriorating snowpack in search of mates. At night, the continuous whistles of saw-whet owls are joined by the first chirps of Pacific treefrogs.

By the end of the month, most black and grizzly bears are out of hibernation. With the first flush of green along the watercourses, the caribou leave the high country lichen forests to enjoy the luxuriant and nutritious new growth below. Mountain goats, still on their low-elevation winter ranges, are attracted to any greening vegetation on steep south-facing slopes.

The yellow spikes of skunk cabbage are at their flashy best in April. Although the occasional Indian paintbrush will bloom in a favoured low-elevation site, deciduous trees and shrubs are the main early season bloomers. Pollen-rich male catkins drape the alders, birches, willows and poplars. It takes a sharp eye to spot the tiny stars of flaming red marking the female hazel flowers amidst the pendulous drapery of male catkins.

Recreation

April is a prime month for cross-country and mountaineering skiing in both parks. Daily warming frequently causes afternoon avalanche activity, so many skiers prefer to start their trips at first light and be out of the mountains by noon. On clear nights the temperature frequently dips well below freezing. By morning the snow surface is often quite hard and for a few hours will support the weight of eager walkers, but it still too early to hike seriously anywhere in the two parks. Picnic areas, campgrounds and viewpoints are usually closed throughout April. Staff at the Rogers Pass Information Centre and the Revelstoke park office can provide information.

MAY

Weather

Above freezing temperatures are now normal at all elevations in the parks, and truly warm weather has arrived in the valley bottoms. Rain dominates at all elevations. In the backcountry, huge climax avalanche releases are common, but along the highway, they are less frequent because of the winter-long program of snowpack reduction. On the glaciers, exposed south exposures are showing signs of spring melt.

May Averages	Revelstoke	Rogers Pass	Mt. Fidelity
Daily High (C)	19.7	10.7	7.4
Daily Low (C)	4.9	− 0.2	0.2
Rainfall (mm)	52.3	63.4	59.4
Snowfall (cm)	0	8.4	43.3
Days with Rain or Snow	10	16	17
Max. snow on ground (cm)	0	140	310
Mid-month sunrise (PST)		5.04	
Mid-month sunset (PST)		20.31	

Wildlife and Plants

The ravens, great horned owls and gray jays are feeding young in the nest at a time when most other park birds are just returning from their southern wintering grounds. By the end of May almost every nesting species has returned to the mountains and has set about the yearly reproduction cycle.

The few reptiles inhabiting the parks also are out of hibernation by this time. Northern alligator lizards and garter snakes often can be spotted sunning themselves on exposed rocks during the cool morning hours.

May is probably the best month of the year to see park mammals. Grizzly bears frequently patrol the avalanche paths where they enjoy a rich harvest of early blooming flowers. Black bears may often be spotted along park roadways feasting on early season dandelions. This is also an excellent month to see mountain goats. Look for them on the greening portions of south-facing avalanche slopes.

May is the first month of the spring to feature extensive wildflower shows. Many avalanche paths along the Trans-Canada Highway are covered by colourful mats of avalanche lilies and spring beauties. The broad-leaved trees seem to change colour daily as their buds burst, cloaking the valleys in green.

Recreation

Hiking can now be done on such trails in the Columbia forest zone as Giant Cedars, Skunk Cabbage, Inspiration Woods and Beaver River, but all trails in the high country are still snowbound. Skiing is still usually good at high elevations.

The Summit Road is usually open for the first 8 km. All roadside viewpoints and most picnic areas in both parks are operational. Although Illecillewaet and Loop campgrounds are still snowbound, limited car camping is available in Glacier. Most park services are fully operational by the end of the month.

JOHN G. WOODS

Gray jays, often called Canada jays or whiskey jacks

JUNE

Weather

The summer solstice brings sixteen hours of daylight. Rainfall dominates the precipitation pattern at all elevations. Although the remaining winter snowpack can still rupture under the weakening rays of the June sun, by the end of the month almost all major avalanche activity is over. Melting in the high country continues to expose crevasses on the glaciers, but the upper subalpine is still typically snow covered throughout June.

June Averages	Revelstoke	Rogers Pass	Mt. Fidelity
Daily High (C)	22.3	16.1	− 11.5
Daily Low (C)	8.6	3.5	3.7
Rainfall (mm)	64.8	95.4	112.2
Snowfall (cm)	0	0.2	15.4
Days with Rain or Snow	11	17	17
Max. snow on ground (cm)	0	40	225
Mid-month sunrise (PST)		4.34	
Mid-month sunset (PST)		21.07	

Wildlife and Plants

Young ravens and gray jays are already out of the nest, and most other birds are in the midst of their nesting cycle. June is the best bird-watching month in both parks: all the migrants are back and most are in full song.

JOHN G. WOODS

One of several viewpoints along the Summit Road

Bird watchers will find Skunk Cabbage Trail and the Summit Road excellent locations.

June is mosquito month in the Columbia Mountains, though they are rarely a discomfort except in the lowest-elevation valleys. Bats also have returned to the mountains, attracted by the rich harvest of nocturnal insects.

Although dandelions continue to attract black bears to the highway corridor, many bears follow the retreating snowline up slope and become more difficult to see. June is mating season for both species of bears; the young you see with the sows in June were born in January.

Many large mammals give birth to their young in June including mule deer, white-tailed deer, caribou, moose and mountain goat. This timing takes advantage of the nutritious vegetation green-up.

The open avalanche paths continue to put on their early season flower show, and in the alpine tundra red snow algae bloom in the water-laden snowpack, often turning the remaining snow pink. By the end of the month, most broad-leaved trees in the parks are in full leaf.

Recreation

All highway picnic areas, campgrounds and viewpoints are open by the end of the month. However, the Summit Road in Mount Revelstoke may be closed above 16 km because of persistent snow at the summit. Ambitious cross-country skiers often drive as far as possible on the Summit Road and hike to snowline for their last ski of the season. Hiking opportunities increase throughout June as the snow melts, but it is still too early for serious exploration of the parks' trail network. Trails below 1300 m will be generally snow free.

JULY

Weather

The long days of July bring the warmest and driest weather of the year. Although snow can still be found above 1300 m early in the month, most years it has largely left the high country by the end of July. Rainstorms in the valleys are often snowstorms on the highest peaks, and this summer snow can cause small point avalanches on the high cliffs. Crevasses on the glaciers become more apparent as the sun attacks their covering of winter snow. Melt water from the glaciers causes park rivers to rise to summer flood levels.

July Averages	Revelstoke	Rogers Pass	Mt. Fidelity
Daily High (C)	26.5	19.8	15.4
Daily Low (C)	10.3	5.8	6.8
Rainfall (mm)	56.8	80.4	104.7
Snowfall (cm)	0	0	2.2
Days with Rain or Snow	9	15	14
Max. snow on ground (cm)	0	0	40
Mid-month sunrise (PST)		4.54	
Mid-month sunset (PST)		20.57	

Wildlife and Plants

Many birds now have young in the nest and are busy feeding them. Bird song has decreased greatly by the start of July, and by the end of the month the mountains seem very quiet. This is probably the best month to find some of the birds specializing in high-elevation habitats, such as rosy finches, water pipits and white-tailed ptarmigan.

Bears are less evident during July. Black bears are hard to spot in the dense foliage, and many of the grizzlies have followed the retreating snowline up slope. Mountain goats also have moved to the high country as the snow disappears. Along the highway, the best opportunity to view wildlife is during the first hour after sunrise.

Alpine flowers begin to bloom by late July. The first wave of avalanche lilies and spring beauties sweeps the high country as soon as it becomes snow free. At lower elevations, huckleberries ripen. If the weather is hot and dry in July, forest fires can be a constant possibility. In these mountains, 95 per cent of the fires are started by summer lightning strikes.

Recreation

All park services and facilities open in July. The Summit Road will usually be open to the top sometime this month depending on the weather. Although July is a good hiking month, expect some snow at the highest elevations.

August is wildflower month on Mount Revelstoke

AUGUST

Weather

The low precipitation and high temperature averages for August make it the best month to explore the parks. On the glaciers, the snow melts back to its maximum yearly retreat—the firn line—and the crevasse fields are fully exposed. Hot weather in August promotes both high water levels in park rivers and the possibilities of forest fires.

August Averages	Revelstoke	Rogers Pass	Mt. Fidelity
Daily High (C)	25.3	19.5	15.6
Daily Low (C)	10	5.7	6.8
Rainfall (mm)	41.3	79.1	100.5
Snowfall (cm)	0	0	0.7
Days with Rain or Snow	8	15	14
Max. snow on ground (cm)	0	0	0
Mid-month sunrise (PST)		5.33	
Mid-month sunset (PST)		20.15	

Wildlife and Plants

Bird life is abundant but exceptionally quiet in August. By the latter part of the month a few summer residents such as black swifts and rufous hummingbirds have left the mountains. The best bird watching is usually in the alpine where high-elevation species can be found.

Most mammals are not easily observed during August. A good strategy is to look for them during the earliest hours of the day—within an hour of sunrise. Some adult Columbian ground squirrels, fat from their summer feasting, enter hibernation by the middle of the month. Pikas are active throughout August gathering hay for their winter food supplies.

The first two weeks of August are often the best times to see alpine

Hermit Meadows in early September

flowers in the parks; the Summit Road in Mount Revelstoke park offers excellent displays within easy access. By month's end the wildflower show is over, and subdued hues of dying vegetation await the first snows.

Recreation

August is traditionally the best month of the year for high country hiking, climbing and glacier travel. All visitor services and facilities are in full operation. Although fishing is not a prime activity in most park streams and lakes, this is a good month to angle for small trout in Eva, Miller and the Jade Lakes of Mount Revelstoke park.

SEPTEMBER

Weather

As the days shorten and the nights cool, autumn comes to the Columbias. Rainstorms in the valleys are frequently snowstorms on the peaks. Glaciers have reached their yearly minimum size, and the crevasse fields await the first permanent snow. Park rivers run low and clear. Nighttime cooling and moist air frequently produce valley fog.

September Averages	Revelstoke	Rogers Pass	Mt. Fidelity
Daily High (C)	19	13	9.4
Daily Low (C)	6.7	2.8	2.6
Rainfall (mm)	59.4	103.9	126.4
Snowfall (cm)	0.1	1.9	22.9
Days with Rain or Snow	9	15	16
Max. snow on ground (cm)	0	0	0
Mid-month sunrise (PST)		6.24	
Mid-month sunset (PST)		19.06	

Heather Lake in early September

Wildlife and Plants

September is a time of bird migration in the parks. The majority of species which come here only for the summer—the warblers, flycatchers, swallows and other insect feeders—leave for the south.

Bears feast on the berry crops and fatten in preparation for winter. As they enter the rut, moose and caribou travel widely throughout the mountains. In the Beaver River drainage, the occasional shrill call of a bugling elk penetrates the mountain forests. Many Columbian ground squirrels and hoary marmots enter hibernation this month. Red squirrels can be seen busily stocking their food middens with coniferous tree cones and mushrooms.

If the weather is wet, mushrooms put on their best shows now. Inspiration Woods Trail and Mountain Creek Campground are good places to see the parks' varied display of autumn fungi. Broad-leaved trees turn colour in September and start losing their leaves.

Recreation

If September is not unduly rainy, it can be one of the best months to hike in the parks. All park picnic areas, viewpoints and at least one of the highway campgrounds are open throughout the month.

OCTOBER

Weather

October sees winter firmly ensconced in the high country; above 1300 m snow is permanent by the end of the month. Snow starts to accumulate in the upper reaches of avalanche paths and to obscure the crevasses on glaciers. Park rivers flow low and clear unless swollen by a mild rainstorm sweeping through the mountains.

October Averages	Revelstoke	Rogers Pass	Mt. Fidelity
Daily High (C)	10.3	4.8	3.1
Daily Low (C)	2.7	− 1.5	− 2.7
Rainfall (mm)	82.4	83.7	49.8
Snowfall (cm)	0.5	48.9	117.5
Days with Rain or Snow	11	18	19
Max. snow on ground (cm)	0	10	49
Mid-month sunrise (PST)		7.15	
Mid-month sunset (PST)		17.54	

Wildlife and Plants
The majority of bird life has left the mountains. Occasional flocks of migrating geese and ducks land briefly on park ponds and lakes. Year-round residents such as ravens, gray jays and chickadees become the most conspicuous birds. On a single drive along the Trans-Canada Highway through Glacier and Mount Revelstoke, you sometimes will see more than fifty Steller's jays in scattered groups of a few birds each.

By the end of the month, all ground squirrels and marmots have entered hibernation as have most black and grizzly bears. Early snows drive mountain goats to lower elevations; look for them above the park snowsheds. Snowshoe rabbits, short-tailed weasels and white-tailed ptarmigan are in colour transition from summer browns to winter whites.

Deciduous trees have all lost their leaves by the end of October as the plant world enters a period of dormancy.

Recreation
If the parks enjoy a period of Indian summer, the hiking season can extend partway into October. Cross-country skiers eager for their first taste of sport can hike to snowline on Mount Revelstoke's Summit Road. As the snow descends downslope the Summit Road is progressively closed at lower elevations. Although park picnic areas and viewpoints are kept open until Thanksgiving Day if possible, highway camping is often limited.

NOVEMBER
Weather
Winter comes to the Columbias in November, and by month's end all elevations have snow on the ground. The avalanche paths reaching the Trans-Canada Highway become active as snows deeply bury critical trigger points. On the glaciers, crevasses disappear as the snow accumulates.

Abbott Snow Research Field Station

November Averages	Revelstoke	Rogers Pass	Mt. Fidelity
Daily High (C)	3.2	− 2.9	− 3.6
Daily Low (C)	− 2	− 7.1	− 8.3
Rainfall (mm)	37.1	20.6	4.9
Snowfall (cm)	51.1	154.3	223.7
Days with Rain or Snow	13	20	21
Max. snow on ground (cm)	16	60	125
Mid-month sunrise (PST)		7.04	
Mid-month sunset (PST)		16.04	

Wildlife and Plants

On occasional years of abundant cone crops, thousands of winter finches invade the Columbia Mountains in November. Most other bird life is inconspicuous, though during the first weeks of the month, for some unknown reason, small groups of Steller's jays line the highways.

With the first persistent snows, most insect life becomes dormant. However, a few specialized "snow insects" such as snow craneflies, snow scorpionflies and glacier crawlers can be seen marching across the sub-zero snows.

Snow mushroom in Woolsey Creek valley

This is the breeding season for white-tailed deer, mule deer and mountain goats. Caribou move down into the valleys to escape the soft new snow at high elevations, but except for tracks across the fresh snow, most evidence of park mammals is hidden from view.

Recreation
In a snowy year, cross-country skiing and ski mountaineering will be good by the end of November. With the start of the avalanche control season, all winter safety regulations come into effect. The Illecillewaet campground remains open on a hike-in-only basis. Check at the Rogers Pass Information Centre or park offices for information.

DECEMBER

Weather
The days have now shortened to a brief eight hours of daylight. Heavy snow accumulations at all elevations establish the winter snowpack, and you can expect heavy avalanche activity this month. Snow blankets the glaciers, filling the crevasses and making them difficult to spot.

Sunrise from a Mount Revelstoke snow cave

JOHN G. WOODS

December Averages	Revelstoke	Rogers Pass	Mt. Fidelity
Daily High (C)	– 1.8	– 6.9	– 7.1
Daily Low (C)	– 6.2	–11.6	–11.8
Rainfall (mm)	28.7	11.1	4
Snowfall (cm)	139.0	236.2	299.9
Days with Rain or Snow	17	23	24
Max. snow on ground (cm)	40	120	200
Mid-month sunrise (PST)		7.47	
Mid-month sunset (PST)		15.43	

Wildlife and Plants

December is a very poor month for bird watching; the days are short and only a few resident species are left in the mountains. Look for American dippers in the parks where they often concentrate along stretches of open water at lower elevations. Their bright song is especially welcome at this unlikely time of the year.

The most visible species of snow invertebrates are the craneflies, gnats, midges, snowfleas, scorpionflies and spiders which stalk the soft December snows.

December is a month of slow starvation for most large mammals in the parks. Deep snows severely hamper their movements and add to their stress. Caribou are an exception. Supported on huge hooves, they can walk across the deep snow after it has had a chance to settle. By the end of the month, these animals are usually to be found in the subalpine where they subsist throughout this hostile period on a diet of carbohydrate-rich tree lichens.

Recreation

In a snowy year, good cross-country skiing and ski mountaineering is possible in December. Although no highway camping is available in the parks, Illecillewaet Campground is kept open on a ski-in basis. Avalanche control is in full operation in December, and all winter safety regulations apply.

SUGGESTED READING

Banfield, A. W. *The Mammals of Canada*. Toronto: University of Toronto Press, 1974.

Berton, Pierre. *The National Dream & The Last Spike*. Toronto: McClelland and Stewart, 1974.

Cavell, Edward. *Legacy in Ice: the Vaux Family in the Canadian Alps*. Banff: Whyte Foundation, 1983.

Daffern, Tony. *Avalanche Safety for Skiers and Climbers*. Calgary: Rocky Mountain Books, 1983.

Fraser, Colin. *Avalanche Enigma*. London: John Murray, 1966.

Fraser, Esther. *Wheeler*. Banff: Summerthought, 1983.

Green, William S. *Among the Selkirk Glaciers*. London: Macmillan, 1890.

Hart, E. J. *The Selling of Canada*. Banff: Altitude Publishing, 1983.

Kariel, Dr. Herbert G. and Kariel, Patricia E. *Alpine Huts in the Rockies, Selkirks and Purcells*. Banff: Alpine Club of Canada, 1986.

Lavallée, Omer. *Van Horne's Road*. Montreal: Railfare, 1974.

Lyons, C. P. *Trees, Shrubs and Flowers to Know in British Columbia*. Vancouver: J. M. Dent and Sons, 1974.

Mark, D. M. *Where to Find Birds in British Columbia*. New Westminster: Kestrel Press, 1978.

Palmer, Howard. *Mountaineering and Exploration in the Selkirks*. New York: G. P. Putnam's Sons, 1914.

Above Rogers Pass on Mount Tupper

Peterson, Roger Tory. *A Field Guide to Western Birds*. Boston: Houghton Mifflin Company, 1969.

Price, R. A., Monger, R. W. H. and Roddick, J. A. "Cordilleran Cross-Section Calgary to Vancouver." In *Field Guides to Geology and Mineral Deposits in the Southern Canadian Cordillera*. Ed. by Dirk Tempelman-Klast. Vancouver: Geological Survey of Canada, 1985.

Putnam, William L. *A Climber's Guide to the Interior Ranges of British Columbia—North*. New York: American Alpine Club, 1975.

——— *The Great Glacier and Its House*. New York: American Alpine Club, 1982.

Soper, J. H. and Szczawinski, A. F. *Mount Revelstoke National Park Wildflowers*. Ottawa: National Museums of Canada, 1976.

Wheeler, Arthur O. *The Selkirk Range,* Ottawa: Government Printing Bureau, 1905.

Woods, John G. *Snow War: An Illustrated History of Rogers Pass*. Ottawa: National and Provincial Parks Association, 1985.

INDEX

To protect for all time those places which are significant examples of Canada's natural and cultural heritage and also to encourage public understanding, appreciation and enjoyment of this heritage in ways which leave it unimpaired for future generations.
Parks Canada mandate

Some of Canada's most beautiful landscapes are protected today in its system of national parks. The high alpine of the Continental Divide. The mist-shrouded beaches of the Atlantic. The rolling grasslands of the Great Plains and the icy expanse of the high Arctic. Each of these landscapes invites exploration, discovery and contemplation; each is represented today in the national park system, part of our collective Canadian heritage. To date, thirty-one national parks have been created by Canadian Parliament, at least one in every province and territory in the country.

The struggles and achievements of those who settled this land are remembered in Canada's system of national historic parks and sites. More than 1000 years of Canadian history are commemorated in seventy-one parks across the country, from the ancient remains of a Viking settlement in L'Anse aux Meadows, Newfoundland, to the reconstruction of a Klondike gold rush town in Dawson City, Yukon, and from the French fortress of Louisbourg in Nova Scotia to the Hudson's Bay Company fort in Fort Langley, British Columbia. In addition, more than 700 national historic plaques across Canada recall the people, places and events that formed this country.

A century has now passed since legislators first set aside 16 km² (6 square miles) of land near Banff Siding for a small public park. The Canadian park system has grown by leaps and bounds since then, a national legacy and a point of pride for all Canadians. Today, Parks Canada is charged with the responsibility of protecting these special places and ensuring that they will be enjoyed by generations of Canadians to come.

Canada